Congress and Law-Making

Congress and Law-Making

Researching the

Legislative Process

Robert Goehlert

Clio Books

Santa Barbara, California   Oxford, England

Library of Congress Cataloging in Publication Data
Goehlert, Robert U
  Congress and Law-Making

  Includes indexes.
  1. Legal research—United States. 2. Legisla-
tive histories—United States. 3. Legislation—
Research—United States. 4. Legislators—Research
—United States. I. Title.
KF240.G63   328.73'07'7072   79-11554
ISBN 0-87436-294-6

American Bibliographical Center—Clio Press
2040 Alameda Padre Serra, Box 4397
Santa Barbara, California 93103

Clio Press, Ltd.
Woodside House, Hinksey Hill
Oxford, OX1 5BE, England

Manufactured in the United States of America

Contents

List of Illustrations   *vii*

The Legislative Process   **1**

Researching Congress   **23**

    Congressional Quarterly Publications   23

    National Journal and American Enterprise Institute for Public
        Policy Research (AEI) Publications   26

    Journals and Newspapers   26

    General Almanacs   30

Tracing Legislation   **31**

    Guides to Congressional Activities   32

    Indexes to Presidential Documents   35

    Guides to Printed Publications of the Legislative Process   38

    Tracing Procedures   42

    Tracing the Privacy Act of 1974   48

Researching Legislators   **61**

    Directories   62

    Election Statistics   67

    Data Archives   72

    Party Strength   75

    Voter Characteristics   76

Campaign Finances   79
Campaign Communication   84
Public Opinion   86
Guides to Statistics   87
Research Centers   88
Library Collections   94
Legislative Research Guides   96

Appendix A: Citing Government Publications   101
Appendix B: Depository Libraries for United States
**   Public Documents   105**
Author Index   158
Title Index   162

List of Illustrations

Table 1. Standing Committees of Congress 2
Table 2. The Legislative Process and Congressional Publications 4
Table 3. A Legislative History of the Privacy Act of 1974 21
Table 4. Guides to Congressional Activities 37

Figure 1. House Bill 7
Figure 2. Senate Bill 8
Figure 3. Senate Committee Hearing 10
Figure 4. Senate Committee Print 11
Figure 5. House Committee Report 13
Figure 6. Senate Committee Report 14
Figure 7. *Congressional Record* 15
Figure 8. Slip Law 16
Figure 9. *U.S. Statutes at Large* 17

Figure 10. *Weekly Compilation of Presidential Documents*   18

Figure 11. *CIS/ANNUAL:* Legislative History   49

Figure 12. *Congressional Record, Daily Digest*: Legislative History   50

Figure 13. *U.S. Code Congressional and Administrative News*: Legislative History   51

Figure 14. *U.S. Statutes at Large*: Legislative History   52

Figure 15. *Digest of Public General Bills and Resolutions*: Legislative History   54

Figure 16. Slip Law: Legislative History   55

The Legislative Process

This guide is designed to help users trace congressional legislation and to familiarize them with the major sources of information about Congress. It provides a basic introduction to the tools of research and how they can be used to gain better insight into Congress and how it works. An understanding of congressional decision-making requires considerable effort and probing, and the tools cited in this guide will require firsthand examination to overcome the bewildering complexity of congressional reference works and bibliographies. There is no substitute for reference tools and diligent research. This guide therefore does not describe at length all the complexities involved in congressional research. It gives the necessary information to begin an independent pursuit of the user's own educational needs. I believe fledgling researchers can proceed on their own course of study once they are equipped with this background information.

When bibliographic citations are not arranged in alphabetical order, the entries are listed according to their usefulness.

The more comprehensive guides and reference works are listed first, followed by those materials that are narrower in scope.

The passage of a bill through Congress is an intricate process, and a full understanding of that process requires a knowledge of law-making procedures and an awareness of such informal influences on congressional decision-making as lobbying and logrolling. The concessions and compromises involved in drafting legislation, some of which take place outside Capitol Hill, are as important as the debates within both chambers of Congress. A description of the formal steps by which a bill becomes law is not a complete picture of the legislative process; however, it is fundamental in tracing legislation. An understanding of the legislative process is necessary to track a law through Congress; a streamlined account of how a bill becomes law follows.

1. A bill is introduced by a member(s) of Congress either in the House or the Senate, except revenue and appropriation bills, which originate in the House.

2. The bill is assigned a number and referred to the committee or committees having jurisdiction over the legislation. Bills are increasingly subject to multiple referrals, which complicates the task of legislative tracing.

Table 1. Standing Committees of Congress

House	Senate
Agriculture	Agriculture, Nutrition, and Forestry
Appropriations	Appropriations
Armed Services	Armed Services
Banking, Finance, and Urban Affairs	Banking, Housing, and Urban Affairs
Budget	Budget
District of Columbia	Commerce, Science, and Transportation
Education and Labor	Energy and Natural Resources
Government Operations	Environment and Public Works
House Administration	Finance
Interior and Insular Affairs	Foreign Relations
International Relations	Governmental Affairs
Interstate and Foreign Commerce	Human Resources
Judiciary	Judiciary
Merchant Marine and Fisheries	Rules and Administration
	Veterans' Affairs

Post Office and Civil Service
Public Works and Transportation
Rules
Science and Technology
Small Business
Standards of Official Conduct
Veterans' Affairs
Ways and Means

3.	The bill is either considered by the committee or refused further study. While in committee, the bill may be amended or even entirely rewritten. Additionally, hearings may be held concerning the ramifications of the bill.

4.	After deliberation by the committee, the bill is submitted to the full chamber. Bills favorably recommended by a committee are accompanied by a report.

5.	The bill is submitted to the floor of the chamber for possible debate on the merits of the legislation. In the house, legislation is brought up on the floor by "privileged status" or by adoption of a "rule" by the Rules Committee; in the Senate, by negotiation or unanimous consent.

6.	If the bill is passed, it is then sent to the other chamber for consideration. Much legislation, however, starts as similar bills in both houses.

7.	The bill undergoes the same process as in the chamber in which it was introduced (steps 2–5).

8.	If the House and Senate versions of the bill differ, the bill is sent into conference, where a compromise is hammered out.

9.	When the bill passes Congress it becomes an act and is sent to the President.

10.	The President either signs the bill and it becomes law or he may veto it. The President has ten days (excepting Sunday) to act upon a bill; if the President does not act within ten days, the bill becomes law without his signature, providing Congress is in session. If Congress adjourns before the ten day limit, the bill does not become law; this is referred to as a "pocket veto."

While there is no philosopher's stone by which one can become adept at legislative tracing, there are some axiomatic principles of tracing which make the undertaking easier. The key is recognizing the relationship between the steps of the legislative process and ensuing congressional publications. It is indispensable to know what publications emanate from each stage of the law-making process. For each level in the legislative process, corresponding publications may exist. For example, when a committee holds hearings, the researcher must automatically try to ascertain if the hearings were published. Table 2 presents legislative steps and the publications that may result from each congressional activity.

Table 2. The Legislative Process and Congressional Publications

Legislative Process	Publications
Bill is Introduced and Referred to Committee	Bills Resolutions
Committee Holds Hearings	Hearings Prints
Committee Recommends Passage	House Reports Senate Reports
Chamber Debates and Votes	*Congressional Record* House/Senate *Journals*
Bill Sent to Conference	Conference Reports
Law	Slip Law *Statutes at Large* *U.S. Code*
Veto	Veto Message
Overriding a Veto	*Congressional Record* House/Senate *Journals*
Presidential Statements	*Weekly Compilation of Presidential Documents*

After becoming familiar with the essential steps in the legislative process, the researcher can start to examine in more detail the precise pathways by which bills journey through Congress.

The researcher, with the steps by which all bills must proceed firmly in mind, can learn through actual tracing some of the variations that may occur in the course of passing legislation.

For additional information, there are several good sources which provide extended treatments and rich background material:

Congressional Quarterly. *Guide to Congress.* 2d ed. Washington, D.C.: Congressional Quarterly, 1976.

Cummings, Frank. *Capitol Hill Manual.* Washington, D.C.: Bureau of National Affairs, 1976.

Oleszek, Walter. *Congressional Procedures and the Policy Process.* Washington, D.C.: Congressional Quarterly, 1976.

Ripley, Randall. *Congress: Process and Policy.* 2d ed. New York: W. W. Norton, 1978.

Zinn, Charles. *How Our Laws Are Made.* Revised and updated by Joseph Fischer. Washington, D.C.: G.P.O., 1978.

The parliamentary procedures used in the House and the Senate can be found in *Rules* and the compilations of prior decisions published by each body:

SENATE

U.S. Congress. Senate. Committee on Rules and Administration. *Senate Manual Containing the Standing Rules, Orders, Laws and Resolutions Affecting the Business of the United States Senate.* Washington, D.C.: G.P.O., 1867–. [Revised biennially.]

U.S. Congress. Senate. *Senate Procedure: Precedents and Practices.* Washington, D.C.: G.P.O., 1974.

HOUSE

U.S. Congress. House. *Constitution, Jefferson's Manual and the Rules of the House of Representatives.* Washington, D.C.: G.P.O., 1797–. [Revised biennially.]

U.S. Congress. House. *Deschler's Precedents of the United States House of Representatives.* Washington, D.C.: G.P.O., 1977.

Hinds, Asher C. *Hinds' Precedents of the House of Representatives of the United States, including Reference to Provisions of the Constitution, the Laws, and Decisions to the United States Senate.* Washington, D.C.: G.P.O., 1907, vols. I–V.

Cannon, Clarence. *Cannon's Precedents of the House of Representatives of the United States, including Reference to Provisions of the Constitution, the Laws, and Decisions of the United States Senate.* Washington, D.C.: G.P.O., 1935–1941, vols. VI–XI.

Almost every textbook on American government will have a chapter on the Congress and a section on how a bill becomes a law. *Government by the People,* by James MacGregor Burns, Jack W. Peltason, and Thomas E. Cronin, is one of the better introductory texts on American politics containing a lucid description of the legislative process. Other good texts include *Democracy under Pressure,* by Milton C. Cummings and David Wise, and *The Politics of American Democracy,* by Marian D. Irish, James W. Prothro, and Richard J. Richardson.

Before one can begin to trace legislation, one must become well versed in the terminology. The following is by no means a complete list, but represents the minimum number of terms one should be able to immediately recognize and understand.

Congress publishes much more than just bills and laws; it disseminates many different kinds of works, including directories, manuals, and legislative calendars. Publications initiated by Congress can be either the product of Congress as a whole or of a particular committee or subcommittee. From the standpoint of legislative tracing, the publications directly resulting from the legislative process are the most significant. They are the documents that accrue as a bill passes through Congress.

Bills and Resolutions are printed versions of a proposed law or resolution as introduced in one or the other house of Congress. Bills are printed and reprinted at various stages of the legislative process. Measures considered by either chamber of Congress include both bills and a variety of resolutions.

Bills are the form used for most legislation, whether permanent or temporary, general or specific, public or private. They may originate in either chamber, except revenue-raising bills, which must be introduced in the House. Appropriations bills, by convention, all originate in the House. Bills introduced in the House are prefixed with H.R., and S. in the Senate. Bills are numbered consecutively as they are introduced from the beginning of each two-year congressional term.

Figure 1. House Bill

93D CONGRESS
2D SESSION

H. R. 16373

IN THE HOUSE OF REPRESENTATIVES

AUGUST 12, 1974

Mr. MOORHEAD of Pennsylvania (for himself, Ms. ABZUG, Mr. ALEXANDER, Mr. BROOMFIELD, Mr. ERLENBORN, Mr. FASCELL, Mr. GOLDWATER, Mr. GUDE, Mr. KOCH, Mr. LITTON, Mr. McCLOSKEY, Mr. MOSS, Mr. THONE, and Mr. WRIGHT) introduced the following bill; which was referred to the Committee on Government Operations

---

A BILL

To amend title 5, United States Code, by adding a section 552a to safeguard individual privacy from the misuse of Federal records and to provide that individuals be granted access to records concerning them which are maintained by Federal agencies.

1   *Be it enacted by the Senate and House of Representa-*

2   *tives of the United States of America in Congress assembled,*

3   That this Act may be cited as the "Privacy Act of 1974".

4   SEC. 2. (a) The Congress finds that—

5   (1) the privacy of an individual is directly affected

6   by the collection, maintenance, use, and dissemination

7   of personal information by Federal agencies;

7

I

Figure 2. Senate Bill

93D CONGRESS
2D SESSION

S. 3418

IN THE SENATE OF THE UNITED STATES

MAY 1, 1974

Mr. ERWIN (for himself, Mr. PERCY, and Mr. MUSKIE) introduced the following bill; which was read twice and referred to the Committee on Government Operations

A BILL

To establish a Federal Privacy Board to oversee the gathering and disclosure of information concerning individuals, to provide management systems in Federal agencies, State, and local governments, and other organizations regarding such information, and for other purposes.

1   *Be it enacted by the Senate and House of Representa-*

2 *tives of the United States of America in Congress assembled,*

3   TITLE I—FEDERAL PRIVACY BOARD

4   ESTABLISHMENT OF BOARD

5   SEC. 101. (a) There is established in the executive

6 branch of the Government the Federal Privacy Board which

7 shall be composed of five members who shall be appointed

8 by the President by and with the advice and consent of the

II

Joint Resolutions are designated H.J. Res. or S.J. Res. A joint resolution goes through the same procedure as a bill and has the force of law. Joint resolutions differ from bills in that they are usually introduced to deal with limited matters, as a single appropriation for a specific objective. Like a bill, a joint resolution requires the approval of both houses and the signature of the President, except when it is used to propose an amendment to the Constitution.

Resolutions are designated H. Res. or S. Res. Often this type of resolution is referred to as "simple resolution." Resolutions concern only the business or sentiments of a single house, and have no legislative effect outside the house in which they originate. The creation and appointment of committees or institution of a special investigation are often results of resolutions. Resolutions become operative upon passage by that house and do not require approval by the other house or the signature of the President.

Concurrent Resolutions are designated H. Con. Res. or S. Con. Res. Concurrent Resolutions are used for matters affecting the business of both houses. They do not require the signature of the President nor do they have the effect of law.

Hearings are designated by an alphanumeric notation known as the SUDOCS (Superintendent of Documents) class number. These contain the oral testimony and written materials submitted to committees of Congress in public sessions held for the purpose of hearing witnesses. Witnesses before hearings include specialists and experts on the subject, important government officials, prominent private citizens, and spokesmen for organizations and groups which may be affected by the bills under consideration.

Committee Prints are also given a SUDOCS classification. These are documents requested by committees which are compiled by their research staffs, outside consultants, or the Congressional Research Service. Committee prints are authorized by a particular committee at the time of a hearing. Used for background information in consideration of a bill, committee prints are often of a technical or research nature. They often contain summaries of staff findings, histories of previous legislation and congressional efforts, and the implications of a bill if it were to be passed.

Figure 3. Senate Committee Hearing

PRIVACY
THE COLLECTION, USE, AND COMPUTERIZATION
OF PERSONAL DATA

JOINT HEARINGS
BEFORE THE
AD HOC SUBCOMMITTEE ON PRIVACY AND INFORMATION SYSTEMS
OF THE
COMMITTEE ON GOVERNMENT OPERATIONS
AND THE
SUBCOMMITTEE ON CONSTITUTIONAL RIGHTS
OF THE
COMMITTEE ON THE JUDICIARY
UNITED STATES SENATE
NINETY-THIRD CONGRESS
SECOND SESSION
ON
S. 3418, S. 3633, S. 3116, S. 2810, S. 2542

JUNE 18, 19, AND 20, 1974

PART 1

Printed for the use of the Committee on Government Operations and the
Committee on the Judiciary

U.S. GOVERNMENT PRINTING OFFICE
37–583 O
WASHINGTON : 1974

Figure 4. Senate Committee Print

| 93d Congress | COMMITTEE PRINT |
| 2d Session | |

MATERIALS PERTAINING TO S. 3418 AND
PROTECTING INDIVIDUAL PRIVACY IN
FEDERAL GATHERING, USE AND
DISCLOSURE OF INFORMATION

———

COMPILED BY STAFF

OF THE

COMMITTEE ON GOVERNMENT OPERATIONS
UNITED STATES SENATE

NOVEMBER 12, 1974

———

U.S. GOVERNMENT PRINTING OFFICE
41–950 O   WASHINGTON : 1974

Not all committee prints are offered to the depository libraries or for sale by the Superintendent of Documents. Often, one
has to request the print directly from the committee or write to
one's legislator. Distribution of committee prints is unpredict-

able, and it is sometimes difficult to obtain prints at all because they are printed in limited pressruns.

Reports are designated H. Rept. or S. Rept. When a committee sends a bill to the floor, it is accompanied by a written report containing the justification for its action. The report explains the scope and purpose of the bill, and includes any amendments or written communications submitted by departments or agencies of the executive branch. A report favors the passage of a bill; a committee does not report its recommendations when it disapproves of a bill. *Report* is used as a noun or a verb. As a noun, *report* refers to the actual document. As a verb, it refers to the process of "reporting a bill," i.e., submitting the committee's findings and recommendations to the parent chamber. Reports are an important element in legislative tracing because they provide an explanation of a bill's intent.

Proceedings include the daily printed debates, statements, and actions taken by each house. The *Congressional Record* is the printed account of the proceedings of both the House and Senate. There are also separate *Journals* for the House and Senate, which are the printed proceedings of each house. These are published at the end of each session.

Conference Reports use the imprint of the chamber where the bill originated, e.g., H.R. 1234. If the two chambers cannot agree on the provisions of a bill, conferees appointed by the House and Senate work to resolve conflicting versions of the bill and hammer out a compromise. When the conferees have harmonized the House and Senate versions of the bill, a conference report is prepared. The compromise bill must then be approved by each house before it is sent to the President.

Slip laws: When a bill has been enacted into law, it is first officially published as a slip law, a separately published law in unbound single-sheet or pamphlet form. Once a bill has received presidential approval, it takes two or three days for the slip law to become available.

Statutes at Large are chronological listing of all the laws enacted by Congress for each session. The laws are indexed by subject and individual.

U.S. Code: The general and permanent laws of the United States are consolidated and codified under fifty titles. The fifty

Figure 5. House Committee Report

93D CONGRESS	HOUSE OF REPRESENTATIVES	REPORT
2d Session		No. 93–1416

PRIVACY ACT OF 1974

OCTOBER 2, 1974.—Committed to the Committee of the Whole House on the State of the Union and ordered to be printed

Mr. MOORHEAD of Pennsylvania, from the Committee on Government Operations, submitted the following

REPORT

together with

ADDITIONAL VIEWS

[To accompany H.R. 16373]

The Committee on Government Operations, to whom was referred the bill (H.R. 16373) to amend title 5, United States Code, by adding a section 552a to safeguard individual privacy from the misuse of Federal records and to provide that individuals be granted access to records concerning them which are maintained by Federal agencies, having considered the same, report favorably thereon with an amendment and recommend that the bill as amended do pass.

The amendment to the text of the bill strikes out all after the enacting clause and inserts a substitute text which appears in italic type in the reported bill.

DIVISIONS OF THE REPORT

Summary and purpose.
Background.
Committee action and vote.
Discussion:
    Definitions.
    Conditions of disclosure.
    Accounting of certain disclosures.
    Access to records.
    Agency requirements.
    Agency rules.
    Civil remedies.
    Rights of legal guardians.
    Criminal penalties.
    General exemptions.

38–006

Figure 6. Senate Committee Report

Calendar No. 1125

93D CONGRESS	SENATE	REPORT
2d Session		No. 93–1181

PRESERVATION, PROTECTION, AND PUBLIC ACCESS
WITH RESPECT TO CERTAIN TAPE RECORDINGS AND
OTHER MATERIALS

SEPTEMBER 26, 1974.—Ordered to be printed

Mr. ERVIN, from the Committee on Government Operations,
submitted the following

REPORT

[To accompany S. 4016]

The Committee on Government Operations, to which was referred
the bill (S. 4016) to protect and preserve recordings of conversations
involving former President Richard M. Nixon and made during his
tenure as President, and for other purposes, having considered the
same, reports favorably thereon with an amendment and recommends
that the bill as amended do pass.

The amendment is in the nature of a substitute.

PURPOSE AND PROVISIONS

The purpose of S. 4016, as amended, is to (1) protect and preserve
tape recordings of conversations, and other materials, recorded or prepared in the White House, the Executive Office Building, and certain
other specified places, between January 20, 1969 and August 9, 1974;
(2) make them available for use by the Special Watergate Prosecution
Force and for access by the public, under regulations promulgated by
the Administrator of General Services who would be required to retain
custody and control of such tapes and other materials; and (3) make
them available to Richard M. Nixon, or his designees, for copying, or
any other purpose, consistent with the Administrator's regulations.

In order to accomplish these objectives, the Committee amendment
directs the Administrator of General Services, notwithstanding the
agreement or understanding he entered into with former President

38–010

14

Figure 7. *Congressional Record*

Congressional Record

United States of America

PROCEEDINGS AND DEBATES OF THE 93ᵈ CONGRESS, SECOND SESSION

Vol. 120 WASHINGTON, THURSDAY, NOVEMBER 21, 1974 *No. 162*

Senate

The Senate met at 12 o'clock meridian and was called to order by the President pro tempore (Mr. EASTLAND).

PRAYER

The Chaplain, the Reverend Edward L. R. Elson, D.D., offered the following prayer:

O Father of our spirits, breathe upon our restless and anxious spirits the calmness of Thy presence and power. In the hush of this hallowed moment, may Earth's strident voices be stilled that Thine alone may be heard in forgiveness and renewal. In the ministry of public affairs as in private life, may we know the psalmist's promise, "He restoreth my soul."

only statutory and Senate rule changes, but constitutional amendments as well. I would venture a guess that more Americans thumbed through the Constitution this year than ever before to seek guidance on the events of the day. Notwithstanding the various tragedies that befell the country, it was refreshing to hear that venerable document being discussed and quoted. We spoke about the 25th amendment dealing with Presidential succession. We spoke about the 22d amendment dealing with the length of Presidential service. And we spoke about article II, section 4, dealing with Presidential impeachment. The public was able to join in the national debate on these questions, and that was a good

Representative John Lindsay noted that a delay in the Senate would put—

The monkey on the back of the Congress to do its job. The President does his job in the selection of a proper person to fill the office of the Vice-Presidency and then Congress must answer to the country if it does not speedily perform its job.

During the congressional impeachment inquiry, I was concerned that the public did not see firsthand what was going on under the Capitol dome. One-sided leaks from whichever side, served no laudable purpose. And printed reports certainly did not give the full story, nor a totally objective one at that. Consequently, the majority leader and I instructed our respective staffs to draw up

Figure 8. Slip Law

Public Law 93-579
93rd Congress, S. 3418
December 31, 1974

𝔄n 𝔄ct

To amend title 5, United States Code, by adding a section 552a to safeguard
individual privacy from the misuse of Federal records, to provide that
individuals be granted access to records concerning them which are maintained
by Federal agencies, to establish a Privacy Protection Study Commission, and
for other purposes.

*Be it enacted by the Senate and House of Representatives of the
United States of America in Congress assembled,* That this Act may
be cited as the "Privacy Act of 1974". | Privacy Act of 1974. 5 USC 552a note.

SEC. 2. (a) The Congress finds that— | Congressional findings. 5 USC 552a note.
   (1) the privacy of an individual is directly affected by the
collection, maintenance, use, and dissemination of personal information by Federal agencies;
   (2) the increasing use of computers and sophisticated information technology, while essential to the efficient operations of
the Government, has greatly magnified the harm to individual
privacy that can occur from any collection, maintenance, use, or
dissemination of personal information;
   (3) the opportunities for an individual to secure employment,
insurance, and credit, and his right to due process, and other legal
protections are endangered by the misuse of certain information
systems;
   (4) the right to privacy is a personal and fundamental right
protected by the Constitution of the United States; and
   (5) in order to protect the privacy of individuals identified in
information systems maintained by Federal agencies, it is necessary and proper for the Congress to regulate the collection, maintenance, use, and dissemination of information by such agencies.
   (b) The purpose of this Act is to provide certain safeguards for an | Statement of purpose.
individual against an invasion of personal privacy by requiring
Federal agencies, except as otherwise provided by law, to—
   (1) permit an individual to determine what records pertaining
to him are collected, maintained, used, or disseminated by such
agencies;
   (2) permit an individual to prevent records pertaining to him
obtained by such agencies for a particular purpose from being
used or made available for another purpose without his consent;
   (3) permit an individual to gain access to information pertaining to him in Federal agency records, to have a copy made of all
or any portion thereof, and to correct or amend such records;
   (4) collect, maintain, use, or disseminate any record of identi-
fiable personal information in a manner that assures that such
action is for a necessary and lawful purpose, that the information is current and accurate for its intended use, and that
adequate safeguards are provided to prevent misuse of such
information;
   (5) permit exemptions from the requirements with respect to
records provided in this Act only in those cases where there is an
important public policy need for such exemption as has been
determined by specific statutory authority; and
   (6) be subject to civil suit for any damages which occur as a
result of willful or intentional action which violates any indi-
vidual's rights under this Act. | 88 STAT. 1896
SEC. 3. Title 5, United States Code, is amended by adding after | 88 STAT. 1897
section 552 the following new section:

Figure 9. *U.S. Statutes at Large*

UNITED STATES
STATUTES AT LARGE

CONTAINING THE

LAWS AND CONCURRENT RESOLUTIONS
ENACTED DURING THE SECOND SESSION OF THE
NINETY-THIRD CONGRESS
OF THE UNITED STATES OF AMERICA

1974

AND

PROCLAMATIONS

VOLUME 88

IN TWO PARTS

PART 2

PUBLIC LAWS 93–447 THROUGH 93–649,
PRIVATE LAWS, CONCURRENT RESOLUTIONS
AND PROCLAMATIONS

UNITED STATES
GOVERNMENT PRINTING OFFICE
WASHINGTON : 1976

Figure 10. *Weekly Compilation of Presidential Documents*

Weekly Compilation of

PRESIDENTIAL
DOCUMENTS

Monday, January 6, 1975

Volume 11 · Number 1

Pages 1-15

titles are arranged by subject, with the first six titles dealing with general subjects and the remaining forty-four titles arranged alphabetically by broad subject area. Every six years the code is revised, and after each session of Congress a supplement is issued.

Presidential Statements: When a President signs or vetos a piece of legislation, he usually issues a brief statement concerning its value or deficiencies. During the time a bill is proceeding through Congress, the President may also make statements concerning the merits of the bill or criticizing or praising Congress for its handling of the bill.

The Serial Set

The Serial Set is a congressional series of publications, selected and compiled under the direction of Congress. Begun in 1789, the Serial Set contains a wealth of information relating to all aspects of congressional activities. The Serial Set, as a whole, constitutes a historical record of the work and accomplishments of the Congress. Included in the Serial Set are documents published by Congress and noncongressional materials originating in executive departments, independent agencies, commissions, and nongovernmental bodies which are required by their incorporation to submit a report to Congress. All documents in the Serial Set, while differing in origin, were printed in the series by reason of their value to the Congress in fulfilling its duties and responsibilities. In general, the Serial Set consists of the following types of publications:

1. Congressional journals
2. Congressional manuals, directories, and other internal documents
3. Congressional reports on public and private bills
4. Special investigatory reports conducted or commissioned by congressional committees
5. Recurring reports to be made to Congress by executive departments and agencies
6. Executive publications ordered by Congress for inclusion
7. Memorial addresses
8. Annual or special reports of nongovernmental bodies required by law to report to Congress

Some of the documents issued in the Serial Set are also sold by the Superintendent of Documents. These documents, such as the *Congressional Directory, House Manual,* and *Senate Manual,* are sold to provide greater distribution to the public.

The best access to Serial Set publications is through Congressional Information Service's *CIS U.S. Serial Set Index.* The twelve-part index covers the period from 1789 to 1969; it includes a comprehensive subject index, an index of names of individuals and organizations who were named as recipients of private relief or related actions of Congress, a numerical list of reports and documents, and a schedule of Serial Set volumes. The *CIS U.S. Serial Set Index* is easy to use, but the Serial Set collection does have a number of idiosyncrasies. Seeking the help of a documents librarian when trying to identify a document will often save time.

The next step is learning how to recognize the specific publications relating to a particular bill. In a sense, appropriate "handles" for identifying documents are needed. For example, the designation H.R. 16373 enables us to isolate a single bill. Just as there is a relationship between the legislative process and publications, there is a connection between publications and the "handles" that identify them. Each publication will have a unique designation, with symbols which will allow us to find documents within a library collection. To illustrate this point, Table 3 provides a legislative history of the Privacy Act of 1974. This history is a profile of how the law traversed through Congress. Later in the text the Privacy Act of 1974 is used to demonstrate how to trace a bill through Congress. Thus Table 3 can serve as a legislative profile the researcher should strive to construct. When actually tracing legislation, it may prove useful to draw up a work sheet similar to Table 3 to record the history of a law. The cover sheets of actual documents are reproduced in Figures 1–10 to help the reader learn what a bill, hearing, report, and law look like in printed form.

**Table 3. A Legislative History of
the Privacy Act of 1974**

History	House	Senate
Bill Number	H.R. 16373	S. 3418
Introduced by	William S. Moorhead Dem., Pa.	Sam J. Ervin, Jr. Dem., N.C.
Date Introduced	Aug. 12, 1974	May 1, 1974
Committee Referred to	Government Operations Committee	Government Operations Committee
Committee Hearings	———	Y4.G74/6:P93/2
Committee Print	———	Y4.G74/6:P93/4
Date Reported	Oct. 2, 1974	Sept. 26, 1974
Report Number	H. Rept. 93-1416	S. Rept. 93-1183
Date of Passage	Dec. 11, 1974	Nov. 21, 1974
Vote in *Congressional Record*	Vol. 120, No. 172, p. H11666	Vol. 120, No. 162, p. S19858
Presidential Statements	*Weekly Compilation of Presidential Documents* Feb. 23, 1974, Vol. 10, No. 8, pp. 245–47 Oct. 9, 1974, Vol. 10, No. 41, p. 1250 Jan. 1, 1975, Vol. 11, No. 1, pp. 7–8 Sept. 29, 1975, Vol. 11, No. 40, pp. 1083–84	
Date Approved	Dec. 31, 1974	
Title of Law	Privacy Act of 1974	
Public Law Number	PL 93-579	
Statutes at Large	88 *Stat.* 1896	
U.S. Code	5 *U.S.C.* 552	
Related Congressional Publications	Y4.G74/6:L52/3; Y4.J89/2:C76/20 Y4.G74/7:R24/7; Y4.G74/7:P93/5	
Related Executive Publications	HE1.2:R24/3; PrEx15.2:P93; Y3.P93/5:2T19 GS4.107/a:P939; Pr37.8:St2/R29	
Background Information	*CQ Almanac* Vol. 30 (1974), pp. 292–94 *CQ Weekly Report,* Vol. 32, No. 39 (Sept. 28, 1974), pp. 2611–14 *National Journal,* Vol. 6, No. 41 (Oct. 12, 1974), pp. 1521–30	

Researching Congress

Congressional Quarterly Publications

Congressional Quarterly is a publisher of voluminous materials on national affairs. Congressional Quarterly reports on all aspects of congressional and executive affairs in publications which have the reputation of being factually reliable and up-to-date. Many Congressional Quarterly publications are relatively inexpensive to acquire. In addition to reference works, Congressional Quarterly issues special paperbacks on current topics and has in print several paperbacks related to Congress, including *Inside Congress, Powers of Congress, Origins and Development of Congress, Impeachment and the U.S. Congress, Members of Congress since 1789*, and *Congressional Districts in the 1970's*. A catalog of publications is available on request from Congressional Quarterly, 1414 22nd St. N.W., Washington, D.C. 20037.

CQ Weekly Report, 1946 –.

Recounts important congressional and political activities for the previous week, including developments in committees as well as on the floor. When covering major pieces of legislation, voting records and excerpts of testimony in hearings are given. Full texts of presidential press conferences, major statements, and speeches are reprinted. Lobbying activities are given considerable coverage, with special reports on the relationship between congressional voting and interest groups. Each issue usually contains an article on special issues or major legislation pending in Congress. The *CQ Weekly Report* quickly publishes the unofficial returns for congressional elections. CQ indexes the *Weekly Report* quarterly and annually. The *Weekly Report* is also indexed in *Public Affairs Information Service Bulletin.*

Congressional Insight, 1976 –.

A weekly newsletter supplementing the *CQ Weekly Report. Congressional Insight* forecasts the outcome of pending bills and summarizes new legislation about to be introduced. *Congressional Insight* is designed to map out what will be happening in Congress in the coming weeks. It reports which bills are ready for action, being ignored, or amended. In an attempt to convey some of the drama of congressional power struggles, *Congressional Insight* focuses on personalities in Congress, discussing their aspirations and conflicts with other legislators, and the roles they play in the battle over a piece of legislation.

CQ Almanac, 1945 –.

Published each spring, the *Almanac* summarizes and cross-indexes the previous year in Congress. Included are accounts of major legislation enacted, analyses of Supreme Court decisions, election results of any federal elections in the last year, an examination of lobbying activities, and other special reports. Like the *CQ Weekly Report,* the *Almanac* records the roll-call vote for every member of Congress.

Congress and the Nation, 1945–1976. 4 vols.

This multivolume reference set spans thirty-one years and six presidential administrations. It is a well-organized reference work providing quick access to descriptions of major legislation, national and international events. The set is an excellent chronological history of major legislative programs and political developments during each Congress and executive administration, including biographical information, major votes, key judicial decisions and election issues. Additional volumes in the series are to be issued at the end of each presidential term.

Guide to Congress. 2d ed., 1976.

This handbook explains how Congress works, beginning with an account of its origins and history. There are chapters on the structure and procedures of Congress and on relations with the other branches of government. The volume is most valuable to the student or researcher who is seeking a basic and thorough understanding of how Congress operates.

Guide to Current American Government, 1968–.
This series serves as a current handbook to developments in the American political system. Issued each spring and fall, it covers the general areas of the presidency, Congress, the judiciary, intergovernmental relations, and lobbies. This series can be used as an up-to-date supplement to both the *CQ Almanac* and *Congress and the Nation.*

Editorial Research Reports, 1923–.
This series follows a journal format and is issued four times a month. The *Reports* provides documented research on the full range of current affairs, from the arts to welfare. Each *Report* attempts to give the reader both the pros and cons on the issue being discussed. Also included are bibliographies for further study. The *Reports* is indexed in *Public Affairs Information Service Bulletin.*

Congressional Roll Call, 1970–.
This special series of CQ publications began with the 1st session of the 91st Congress. Each volume opens with an analysis and legislative description of key votes on major issues, followed by special voting studies such as freshman voting, bipartisanship, voting participation. The remainder of the volume is a member-by-member analysis, in chronological order, of all roll-call votes in the House and Senate. There is also a roll-call subject index. In the compilation of roll-call votes, there is a brief synopsis of each bill, the total vote, and vote-by-party affiliation for each vote. The indexes record whether the member voted for or against, paired for* or against, announced for or against, was polled by CQ as for or against, voted "present," voted "present" to avoid a conflict of interest, or did not vote or make his position known. The voting indexes in the *CQ Weekly Report* and *CQ Almanac* are presented in the same format.

---

*A "gentlemen's agreement" between two opposing legislators to refrain from voting on a roll call so their absence will not affect the decision of a recorded vote in Congress.

National Journal and American Enterprise Institute for Public Policy Research (AEI) Publications

National Journal: The Weekly on Politics and Government. Washington, D.C.: Government Research Corporation, 1969–.

National Journal, a weekly publication, covers all areas of federal decision-making. It provides excellent analyses of congressional activities, including important hearings and all roll-call votes. In some respects *National Journal* is similar to the *CQ Weekly Report,* but it gives more emphasis on developments in the executive branch. Using both *CQ Weekly Report* and *National Journal* will provide excellent coverage of current political events. *National Journal* is self-indexed quarterly and annually by subject, individual, and organization.

AEI, established in 1943, is a nonprofit research and educational organization. The institute publishes studies and analyses on national and international issues, including economics, politics, foreign affairs, and defense. The Legislative Analyses Series summarizes current proposals before Congress, and is especially useful for students. Each year AEI publishes *Review: [year] Session of Congress and Index of AEI Publications.* The annual provides an overview of the past year in Congress, a digest of major laws passed, a summary of congressional action on the budget, and an index to the year's publications.

Journals and Newspapers

In addition to Congressional Quarterly publications, there are sundry other sources of information on congressional politics. The researcher interested in congressional activities will have no difficulty finding materials. Sometimes the problem a researcher faces is settling on a topic and weeding through citations. A substantial amount of information can be found in periodical literature. Journal articles are important because they are published faster than books and often treat narrow topics. Every researcher should learn how to engineer his own literature search, including the use of indexes and abstracting services. While there are many journals containing articles on congressional affairs, the following serial publications regularly include articles about Congress:

American Academy of Political and Social Science, The
    Annals
American Journal of Political Science
American Political Science Review
American Politics Quarterly
Congressional Digest
Congressional Studies
Democratic Review
Focus
Harvard Journal on Legislation
Journal of Politics
Law and Contemporary Politics
Legislative Studies Quarterly
National Journal
Political Science Quarterly
Polity
Public Interest
Review of Politics
Social Science Quarterly
United States Law Week
Washington Monthly
Western Political Quarterly
Women's Political Times

All of the journals listed above are indexed in at least one of the following indexes:

ABC POL SCI
ABS Guide to Recent Literature in the Social and
    Behavioral Sciences
America: History and Life
American Political Science Research Guide
The Federal Index
Index to Legal Periodicals
Index to Periodical Articles Related to Law
Index to U.S. Government Periodicals

> *International Bibliography of Political Science*
> *International Political Science Abstracts*
> *Public Affairs Information Service Bulletin (PAIS)*
> *Social Sciences Citation Index*
> *Social Sciences Index*
> *United States Political Science Documents*
> *Writings on American History*

Since these indexes cover almost all the journals in the field of political science, and a large share of the social sciences periodicals in general, articles can be found in journals from a variety of fields.

The *Federal Index,* published by Predicasts, Inc., indexes the *Washington Post, Congressional Record, Federal Register, Commerce Business Daily,* and Presidential documents. The *Federal Index* can be used to find information about proposed bills, rules, regulations, hearings, reports, roll calls, executive orders, and court decisions. There are other indexes and abstracting services in the social sciences that focus on specific fields, such as urban affairs and administrative and policy studies. Those indexes are particularly useful for finding material on legislative programs and the operations of Congress. The Council of State Governments has published *Suggested List of Periodicals Useful for Legislative Reference Research,* BYU–74 (November, 1974). The Council of State Governments' guide lists 144 periodicals from all fields, noting the price, frequency, where indexed, and the address of the publisher.

Five of the above indexes *(America: History and Life, Federal Index, PAIS, Social Sciences Citation Index,* and *United States Political Science Documents)* are available through Lockheed's DIALOG service for on-line computer searching. More information on DIALOG data bases can be found in *Database Catalog,* which can be obtained by writing to Lockheed or at a library or information center that offers data base searching services.

By using the subject catalog of any large library and the various indexes mentioned, one can quickly find many citations to materials on Congress. There are a few bibliographies on Congress and legislative studies in general which can be used to start one's research and to build upon.

> U.S. Senate Historical Office. *The United States Senate: A Historical Bibliography.* Washington, D.C.: G.P.O., 1977.
> Jones, Charles O., and Randall B. Ripley. *The Role of*

Political Parties in Congress: A Bibliography and Research Guide. Tucson: University of Arizona Press, 1966.

Kerwood, John R., ed. *The United States Capitol: An Annotated Bibliography.* Norman: University of Oklahoma Press, 1973.

Michigan Senate Fellows. *The Legislative Process: A Bibliography in Legislative Behavior.* Lansing: Institute for Community Development, Michigan State University, 1964.

Tomkins, Dorothy L. C. *Congressional Investigation of Lobbying: A Selected Bibliography.* Berkeley: Institute of Governmental Studies, University of California, 1956.

Tomkins, Dorothy L. C. *Changes in Congress.* Berkeley: Institute of Governmental Studies, University of California, 1966.

Wilcox, Allen R. *Voting in Collegial Bodies: A Selected Bibliography.* Reno: Bureau of Governmental Research, University of Nevada, 1971.

Newspapers are unrivaled for their ability to provide almost instantaneous reporting on congressional activities. The uniqueness of newspapers is their daily publication. For tracing legislation in progress, newspapers can provide vivid day-by-day reports. The two best newspapers for following legislation are the *New York Times* (indexed in the *New York Times Index*) and the *Washington Post* (indexed in *The Newspaper Index*). Most local newspapers throughout the country publish the voting records of senators and representatives in their state. Local newspapers regularly feature columns about the activities of legislators when they are back in their home districts and while they are in Washington. Election returns for precincts, wards, towns, and cities can also be found in area newspapers.

NEWSPAPER INDEXES

The New York Times. *The New York Times Index.* New York, 1851–.

Christian Science Monitor. *Index to the Christian Science Monitor.* Ann Arbor, Mich.: University Microfilms, 1959–.

The Wall Street Journal. *The Wall Street Journal Index.* Princeton, N.J.: Dow Jones, 1958–.

The National Observer. *Index.* Flint, Mich.: Newspaper Indexing Center, 1970–.

The Newspaper Index. Wooster, Ohio: Newspaper Indexing Center, Bell and Howell, 1972–. [Indexes the *Los Angeles Times, Chicago Tribune, New Orleans Times-Picayune,* and *Washington Post.*]

California News Index. Claremont: Center for California Public Affairs, 1970–. [Indexes the *Los Angeles Times, San Diego Union, Sacramento Bee, San Francisco Chronicle.*]

The Newsbank Urban Affairs Library. Spring Valley, N.Y.: Arcata Microfilm, 1971–. [Indexes over 150 major newspapers in more than 100 cities.]

General Almanacs

Information Please Almanac. New York: Simon and Schuster, 1947–.

The Official Associated Press Almanac. Maplewood, N. J.: Hammond Almanac, 1974–.

World Almanac and Book of Facts. New York: Newspaper Enterprise Association, 1868–.

These annual publications are useful ready-reference sources. While each of the almanacs uses a different format, they all contain essentially the same information. Election returns since 1789 are given on a national basis, including the electoral vote, popular vote, and sometimes percentages or pluralities. For the most recent elections, results are broken down by state. All of these almanacs often vary from year to year in regard to the data given. Usually almanacs published following an election year include somewhat more detailed statistics, such as election results by county. For quick and easy checking on congressional elections, almanacs should not be forgotten or bypassed in the search for statistics. But for more scholarly research, these sources should only be regarded as the initial step.

Tracing Legislation

We have seen how a bill passes through Congress and the publications that result from the sequence. What has not yet been covered are the tools used to trace a bill through Congress and to identify what publications exist. There are numerous tools, some published by the federal government and others produced by private commercial companies. The concise annotations provided here do not really do justice to these tools, for many of them are considerably complex; but this section is intended to acquaint the user with their existence and purpose. The best way to learn to use these tools fully is to use them repeatedly. The next section of this guide will present various strategies for tracing legislation using these bibliographic guides.

The research tools listed are all currently being published. Several special tools must be used when tracing legislation in the early years of the Republic. More information about these reference handbooks is provided in the "Legislative Research Guides" section (see table of contents).

Tables 2 and 3 show the relationship between the stages of the legislative process and the publications that originate from that progression. When using the tools, remember the distinction between guides to legislative action and guides to printed publications. A guide to legislative action allows the user to reconstruct a history of a bill's passage through Congress, i.e., to find the date it was introduced, referred to committee, reported to chamber, voted upon, etc. Guides to printed publications enable the user to identify the citations necessary for finding the documents related to the bill being researched. Many tools do both; the *Congressional Record* is both a guide to legislative action and an index to the floor proceedings which it actually contains. The distinction is useful, however, because it reminds the user to first trace the steps of a law and then find specific citations to publications.

Tracing legislation means being a detective. Like any good sleuth, the legal researcher is busy uncovering clues to crack his case. The evidence he is seeking lies in the guides to legislative action and publications. The development of a legislative history is analogous to the piecing together of the events surrounding a crime. In his mind, the detective keeps notes of where and when everyone was involved. When all the researcher's evidence has been gathered, he can reconstruct a legislative history, showing exactly how and when a bill progressed through Congress.

Guides to Congressional Activities

Congressional Index. Washington, D.C.: Commerce Clearing House, 1937/38–. [Weekly.]
   Indexes congressional bills and resolutions and lists their current status. The index is designed to enable the user to follow the progress of legislation from introduction to final disposition; it contains a section on voting records

in which all roll-call votes are reported. The guide provides a sequential history of legislation and is a good tool for following a bill through Congress. Vetoes and subsequent congressional actions are recorded.

U.S. Library of Congress, Congressional Research Service. *Digest of Public General Bills and Resolutions.* Washington, D.C.: G.P.O., 1935–.
Normally published each session in five cumulative issues with biweekly supplements. The *Digest* provides a brief synopsis of public bills and resolutions and records the introduction of a bill or resolution, committee referred to, and last action taken. Arrangement is by bill number; the *Digest* includes a subject index.

Congressional Record: Proceedings and Debates of the Congress. Washington, D.C.: G.P.O., 1873–.
A daily record of the proceedings of Congress, including a history of legislation. Consists of four sections: (1) proceedings of the House, (2) proceedings of the Senate, (3) extensions and remarks, and (4) the "Daily Digest" of the activities of Congress. The proceedings are indexed by subject and individual. The "History of Bills and Resolutions" section is arranged by bill and resolution number. While the *Congressional Record* provides a sequential history, it does not provide as much information as the *Congressional Index.* Consequently, the *Congressional Index* is often easier to use. The *Congressional Record* is important for finding roll-call votes and congressional action on vetoed bills.

The *Congressional Record* is not a literal transcription of the floor debates. Legislators or their staffs have a chance to edit it before it goes into print, and again before it goes into the bound volume. The daily edition is therefore somewhat more accurate than the bound volume. Normally this distinction makes little difference; but in hard-fought debates, as in final passage of legislation, there may be considerable editing.

U.S. Congress. House. *Journal.* Washington, D.C.: G.P.O., 1789–.

U.S. Congress. Senate. *Journal.* Washington, D.C.: G.P.O., 1789–.

These are the official minutes of Congress, published at the end of a session. Both *Journals* have a "History of Bills and Resolutions," in which legislative actions are arranged by number, title, and action. The *Journals* each have a name, subject, and title index. Prior to the publication of the *Congressional Record,* the floor proceedings were published in the *Annals of Congress, Register of Debates in Congress,* and the *Congressional Globe.*

Records of Floor Proceedings

1789–1824	*Annals of the Congress of the United States.* Washington, D.C.: Gales and Seaton, 1834–1856.
1824–1837	*Register of Debates in Congress.* Washington, D.C.: Gales and Seaton, 1825–1837.
1833–1873	*The Congressional Globe.* Washington, D.C.: Congressional Globe, 1835–1873.
1873–present	U.S. Congress. *Congressional Record.* Washington, D.C.: G.P.O., 1874–.
1789–present	U.S. Congress. Senate. *Journal of the Senate of the United States of America.* Washington, D.C.: G.P.O., 1789.
1789–present	U.S. Congress. House. *Journal of the House of Representatives of the United States of America.* Washington, D.C.: G.P.O., 1789–.
1828–present	*Journal of the Executive Proceedings of the Senate of the United States of America.* Washington, D.C.: G.P.O., 1828–.

U.S. Congress. House. *Calendars of the United States House of Representatives and History of Legislation.* Washington, D.C.: G.P.O., 1951–.

Published daily when the House is in session; each issue is cumulative. Appearing in the Monday issue is a subject index to all legislative action to date in both the House and Senate. House and Senate bills passed or pending are arranged numerically in a table. Because this series is cumulative it is a useful guide to legislative action.

Congressional Monitor. Washington, D.C.: Washington Monitor, 1965–.

The *Congressional Monitor* is published each day Congress is in session. Each issue provides committee actions and witnesses scheduled for the day. A "Weekly Legislative Status Report" is issued every Friday, and bills are indexed by bill number. This is the fastest reporting service covering congressional action. The Washington Monitor also publishes *Congress in Print: A Weekly Alert to Just-Released Committee Hearings, Prints and Staff Studies,* which provides an up-to-the-minute listing of new publications.

*United States Statutes at Large: Containing the Laws and Concurrent Resolutions Enacted. . . .*Washington, D.C.: G.P.O., 1789–.

A record of all laws, published in their final form, giving the full text of congressional acts and resolutions passed during a congressional session. Slip laws, i.e., the texts of individual acts, are published separately as they are passed. Slip laws give legislative histories on the inside back cover and are indexed in the *Monthly Catalog of United States Government Publications.* Since 1963 the *Statutes at Large* contains a section entitled "Guide to Legislative History of Bills Enacted into Public Law."

United States Code. Washington, D.C.: G.P.O., 1926–.

A compilation of all federal laws in force. The laws are arranged by subject under fifty "titles." The index volume contains a table of all title and chapter headings and a subject index to all sections. The Office of the Federal Register has published two useful guides which are helpful for learning how to use the *Statutes* and *Code: How to Find U.S. Statutes and U.S. Code Citations* (3d rev. ed., 1977); *The Federal Register: What It Is and How to Use It; A Guide for the User of the Federal Register-Code of Federal Regulations System* (1978).

Indexes to Presidential Documents

United States Code Congressional and Administrative News. St. Paul, Minn.: West Publishing, 1939–. [Monthly.]

Reprinting the full text of all public laws, this series reproduces the *U.S. Statutes at Large*. But this service also provides information on the status of legislation, contained in seven tables. One of the tables provides a complete legislative history of all bills passed as law. As the series is cumulative, it is an excellent tool for legislative tracing.

Weekly Compilation of Presidential Documents. Washington, D.C.: G.P.O., 1965–.

Published every Monday to cover the preceding week. An up-to-date source of information which includes the full text of messages, speeches, press conferences, executive orders, and statements by the President. All bills signed or vetoed are listed. A cumulative index is published with each issue.

Public Papers of the President of the United States. Washington, D.C.: U.S. National Archives and Records Administration, 1958–.

Published annually, the text of the volumes include oral and written statements of the President. Materials are selected from communications to Congress, public speeches, press conferences, public letters, messages to heads of states, and executive documents. This series is edited, thus some discrepancies exist between the *Public Papers* and *Weekly Compilation of Presidental Documents*. KTO Press has published *The Cumulated Indexes to the Public Papers of the Presidents*. At present the five-volume set spans the Truman to Nixon presidencies. KTO Press expects to issue volumes as each President's administration is completed. Besides containing the texts of documents, each volume indexes the complete public papers of a presidential administration. Formerly, it was necessary to use each individual volume of the government's annual series, *The Public Papers of the Presidents of the United States*.

Presidential Vetoes, 1789–1976. Washington, D.C.: G.P.O., 1978.

A handy reference work listing vetoes chronologically by congressional session and presidential administration. The vetoes are entered by bill number and include the citation to the *Congressional Record* where the message is printed.

Table 4 summarizes the relationship between the legislative process and the tools best suited for tracing those steps.

Table 4. Guides to Congressional Activities

Legislative Process	Guides to Legislative Action
Bill is Introduced and Referred to Committee	*CQ Weekly Reports* *CIS/INDEX* *Congressional Index* *Congressional Record* *Digest of Public General Bills and Resolutions* *National Journal*
Committee Holds Hearings	*CQ Weekly Report* *CIS/INDEX* *Congressional Index* *Congressional Monitor* *Congressional Record* *National Journal*
Committee Recommends Passage	*CQ Weekly Report* *CIS/INDEX* *Calendars of House and History of Legislation* *U.S. Code Congressional and Administrative News* *Congressional Index* *Congressional Monitor* *Congressional Record* *National Journal*
Chamber Debates	*CQ Weekly Report* *Congressional Record* *Congressional Monitor* *Congressional Index* *National Journal*
Chamber Votes	*CQ Weekly Report* *CIS/INDEX* *CQ Almanac* *Congressional Index* *Congressional Record* *Congressional Roll Call* House *Journal* *National Journal* Senate *Journal*
Bill is Sent to Conference	*CQ Weekly Report* *CIS/INDEX* *Calendars of House and History of Legislation* *U.S. Code Congressional and Administrative News* *Congressional Index* *Congressional Monitor* *Congressional Record* *National Journal*

Table 4. Guides to Congressional Activities

Legislative Process	Guides to Legislative Action
Presidential Statements	*CQ Weekly Report* *CIS/INDEX* *National Journal* *Public Papers of the President* *Weekly Compilation of Presidential Documents*
Law	*CQ Weekly Report* *CIS/INDEX* *Congressional Index* *Calendars of House and History of Legislation* *CQ Almanac* *Congressional Record* *Digest of Public General Bills and Resolutions* *National Journal* *Statutes at Large* *U.S. Code*
Veto	*CQ Weekly Report* *CIS/INDEX* *Congressional Index* *Calendars of House and History of Legislation* *CQ Almanac* *Congressional Record* *Monthly Catalog* *National Journal* *Public Papers of the President* *Weekly Compilation of Presidential Documents* *Presidential Vetoes*
Overriding a Veto	*CQ Weekly Report* *CIS/INDEX* *CQ Almanac* *Congressional Index* *Congressional Record* House *Journal* *Congressional Roll Call* *National Journal* Senate *Journal*

Guides to Printed Publications of the Legislative Process

CIS/INDEX: Congressional Information Service/Index to Publications of the United States Congress. Washington,

D.C.: Congressional Information Service, 1970—. [Monthly.]

An inclusive index to congressional publications. It abstracts all publications emanating from the legislative process. Materials are indexed by subject, individual, committees, bill numbers, report numbers, document numbers, and names of committee chairmen. Because *CIS/INDEX* abstracts reports, hearings, and other congressional documents, the researcher can save valuable time by reading the synopses of publications. For many researchers, *CIS/INDEX* is the first place to look when tracing legislation. There are quarterly cumulative indexes, and at the end of the year the CIS/ANNUAL is issued. There is also the *CIS Five-Year Cumulative Index, 1970–1974.* A guide to using *CIS/INDEX,* the *CIS/INDEX User Handbook,* is available in most libraries which subscribe to *CIS/INDEX,* or it can be obtained from the Congressional Information Service. A *CIS/INDEX* data base is also available on-line through ORBIT (System Development Corporation) for computer searching.

Monthly Catalog of United States Government Publications. Washington, D.C.: G.P.O., 1895–.

An important index for identifying many congressional publications, the *U.S. Monthly Catalog* is especially useful for finding committee hearings and reports. It has a subject index as well as an index arranged by government author. Carrollton Press has published *Cumulative Subject Index to the Monthly Catalog of United States Government Publications, 1900–1971.*

GPO Sales Publication Reference File. Washington, D.C.: G.P.O., 1977–.

The *Publication Reference File* is a "documents in print;" it catalogs all federal publications currently sold by the Superintendent of Documents. Documents are arranged by subject, title, agency series and report numbers, key word, author, stock number, and SUDOCS classification number. The *PRF* is issued on 48X microfiche and is available to depository libraries. The *PRF* is easy to use and is the first place to look to identify new documents.

Bibliographic Guide to Government Publications: U.S. Boston: G. K. Hall, 1975–.

This guide lists documents cataloged by the Research **39**

Libraries of the New York Public Libraries and by the Library of Congress. The annual editions serve as a supplement to the *Catalog of Government Publications of the Research Libraries of the New York Public Libraries* (40 vols., G. K. Hall, 1972).

Public Affairs Information Service Bulletin. New York: The Service, 1915–. [Weekly.]

A subject guide to American politics in general, indexing government publications, books, and periodical literature. It includes citations to many hearings, and it indexes *National Journal, CQ Weekly Report, Congressional Digest* and, selectively, the *Weekly Compilation of Presidential Documents.* All of these journals are invaluable guides to legislative action on a current basis. A fifteen-volume *Cumulative Subject Index to the P.A.I.S. Annual Bulletins, 1915–1974* is being published by Carrollton Press. *PAIS* is cumulated quarterly and annually.

Cumulative Index of Congressional Committee Hearings. Washington, D.C.: G.P.O., 1935–.

The *Cumulative Index* and its supplements can be used for tracing hearings prior to the publication of *CIS/ INDEX.* The *Cumulative Index* provides access by bill number, subject, and committee. Greenwood Press has published on microfiche *Witness Index to the United States Congressional Hearings 25th–89th Congress (1839–1966).*

INDEXES OF COMMITTEE HEARINGS

1839–1935	Thomen, Harold O. *Supplement to the Index of Congressional Hearings Prior to January 3, 1935, Consisting of Hearings Not Catalogued by the U.S. Senate Library, from the Twenty-Fifth Congress, 1839, through the Seventy-Third Congress, 1934.* Westport, Conn.: Greenwood Press, 1973.
Prior to 1935	U.S. Congress. Senate. Secretary of the Senate. *Index of Congressional Committee Hearings (Not Confidential in Character) prior to January 3, 1935, in the United States Senate Library.* Westport, Conn.: Greenwood Press, 1971. [Reprinted from 1935 edition.]

Prior to 1951 | U.S. Congress. House. Clerk of the House of Representatives. *Index to Congressional Committee Hearings in the Library of the United States House of Representatives prior to January 1, 1951.* Washington, D.C.: G.P.O., 1954.

1935–1959 | U.S. Congress. Senate. Secretary of the Senate. *Cumulative Index of Congressional Committee Hearings (Not Confidential in Character) from Seventy-Fourth Congress (January 3, 1935) through Eighty-Fifth Congress (January 3, 1959) in the United States Senate Library.* Westport, Conn.: Greenwood Press, 1973. [Reprinted from 1959 edition.]

1959–present | U.S. Congress. Senate. Secretary of the Senate. *Quadrennial Supplements to Cumulative Index of Congressional Committee Hearings (Not Confidential in Character): Quadrennial Supplement, together with Selected Committee Prints in the United States Senate Library.* Washington, D.C.: G.P.O., 1963.

INDEXES OF COMMITTEE PRINTS

1911–1969 | *A Bibliography and Indexes of United States Congressional Committee Prints: From the Sixty-First Congress, 1911, through the Ninety-First Congress, First Session, 1969, in the United States Senate Library.* Edited by Rochelle Field, compiled by Gary Halvarson et al. 2 vols. Westport, Conn.: Greenwood Press, 1976.

1917–1969 | *A Bibliography and Indexes of United States Congressional Committee Prints: From the Sixty-Fifth Congress, 1917, through the Ninety-First Congress, First Session, 1969, Not in the United States Senate Library.* Edited by Rochelle Field, compiled by Laura J. Kaminsky, Gary Halvarson, and Mark Woodbridge. Westport, Conn.: Greenwood Press, 1977.

Tracing Procedures

You will not be confident you are using the best strategy until you have worked through several legislative tracing exercises. Often a researcher is not sure where to start or becomes lost somewhere in the process. The following outlines are designed to guide you through legislative tracing step by step. The key to legislative tracing is attaining a bill's or statute's number. Once you have that number, it is relatively easy to compile a legislative history and identify all relevant documents. The other major way of tracing legislation is by subject. But it is sometimes best to isolate a group of bills on a particular subject and trace the bills by their numbers.

To get the bill or statute number is not a difficult task. Because most of the guides to legislative action are indexed in a variety of ways (names of individuals, committees, report numbers, etc.), a single piece of information about a bill or law can be used to identify their number. Knowing who introduced a bill or to which committee it was referred can lead to the bill or statute number. If no specific information about a bill or law is known, it becomes necessary to use a subject approach. The subject indexing in the guides are quite good. Even if one has only a general knowledge of the substance of a bill or statute, a subject index will lead to their numbers.

RETROSPECTIVE TRACING

These are the steps to follow if a bill has already been passed into law.

1. Get statute number.
2. Go to any of the following indexes to get the legislative history:
   CQ Almanac or *CQ Weekly Report*
   CIS/ANNUAL—"Index of Bill, Report and Document Numbers"
   U.S. Code Congressional and Administrative News—"Table of Legislative History"

Congressional Record, Daily Digest—"History of
   Bills Enacted into Law"
Digest of Public General Bills and Resolutions—
   "Public Law Listing"
*Calendars of the House and History of
   Legislation*—"Index Key and History of Bill"
Statutes at Large—"Guide to Legislative History of
   Bills Enacted into Public Law"
House *Journal*—"History of Bills and Resolutions"
Senate *Journal*—"History of Bills and Resolutions"
Slip Law—"Legislative History"

3. If the statute number is not known, go to the subject,
   author, or other category indexes in the following
   guides to get the statute number:
   CIS/ANNUAL
   Congressional Index
   Congressional Record
   CQ Almanac
   Calendars of House and History of Legislation
   Digest of Public General Bills and Resolutions
   Statutes at Large
   U.S. Code Congressional and Administrative News
   House *Journal*
   Senate *Journal*

4. Find and examine the publications issued by both
   houses.
   Bills and resolutions can be traced through:
   CIS/ANNUAL
   Congressional Index
   Congressional Record
   CQ Almanac
   Digest of Public General Bills and Resolutions
   Calendars of House and History of Legislation
   Hearings and committee prints can be traced
   through:
   CIS/ANNUAL
   *Monthly Catalog of U.S. Government
      Publications*
   Public Affairs Information Service Bulletin
   *Cumulative Index of Congressional Committee
      Hearings*

Cumulative Subject Index to the Monthly Catalog
House, Senate, and conference report numbers can
   be traced through:
CIS/ANNUAL
Congressional Record
Congressional Index
Calendars of House and History of Legislation
*U.S. Code Congressional and Administrative
   News*
*Monthly Catalog of U.S. Government
   Publications*
Cumulative Subject Index to the Monthly Catalog
Proceedings and debates of Congress are fully
   indexed in:
Congressional Record
Senate *Journal*
House *Journal*
Roll call votes are recorded in:
CQ Almanac
Congressional Roll Call
CQ Weekly Report
National Journal
Congressional Record
Congressional Index
Senate *Journal*
House *Journal*
Presidential statements are printed and indexed
   in:
Weekly Compilation of Presidential Documents
Public Papers of the President
*Cumulated Indexes to the Public Papers of the
   Presidents*
Laws are printed in:
*U.S. Code Congressional and Administrative
   News*
Statutes at Large
U.S. Code
Veto messages are printed in:
Weekly Compilation of Presidential Documents
Congressional Record
House *Journal*
Senate *Journal*

Congressional votes on vetoes are recorded in:
CQ Weekly Report
National Journal
Congressional Record
Congressional Index
Senate *Journal*
House *Journal*
CQ Almanac
Congressional Roll Call
5. For analysis and commentary of legislation, proceed to:
CQ Almanac
National Journal
U.S. Code Congressional and Administrative News
Public Affairs Information Service Bulletin

CURRENT TRACING

When tracing legislation which has been introduced and is in the process of becoming law, follow these steps, which will lead to a complete legislative history once the bill becomes law:
1. Get bill number.
2. Go to the following guides to determine the present status of the bill:
CQ Weekly Report
Congressional Index—"Status Tables"
Digest of Public General Bills and Resolutions—"Status Table"
Congressional Record—"History of Bills and Resolutions"
CIS/INDEX—"Index of Bill, Report, and Document Numbers"
Calendars of House and History of Legislation—"Index Key and History of Bill"
U.S. Code Congressional and Administrative News—"Public Laws Table"
3. If the bill number is not known, go to the subject, author, or other category indexes in the following guides to determine the bill number:
CIS/INDEX
CQ Weekly Report
Congressional Index

Congressional Record
Calendars of House and History of Legislation
Digest of Public General Bills and Resolutions
4. Follow the bill through Congress recording what actions transpired and what publications were issued.
Committee activities and publications, hearings and prints, can be traced through:
CIS/INDEX
CQ Weekly Report
National Journal
Congressional Monitor
Public Affairs Information Service Bulletin
Monthly Catalog of U.S. Government Publications
Committee report numbers can be found in:
CIS/INDEX
CQ Weekly Report
National Journal
Congressional Index
Calendars of House and History of Legislation
Congressional Record
Monthly Catalog of U.S. Government Publications
U.S. Code Congressional and Administrative News
Floor proceedings and debates can be followed through:
Congressional Record
CQ Weekly Report
National Journal
Congressional Monitor
Congressional Digest
Roll-call votes are recorded in:
CQ Weekly Report
National Journal
Congressional Record
Congressional Index
Presidential statements are referenced in:
Weekly Compilation of Presidential Documents
CQ Weekly Report
National Journal
Slip law approval is recorded in:
CIS/INDEX

CQ Weekly Report
National Journal
Congressional Record
Congressional Index
Calendars of House and History of Legislation
U.S. Code Congressional and Administrative News
Congressional Monitor
Veto messages are referenced in:
CIS/INDEX
CQ Weekly Report
Congressional Record
Calendars of House and History of Legislation
Weekly Compilation of Presidential Documents
Monthly Catalog of U.S. Government Publications
Congressional votes on vetoes are recorded in:
CQ Weekly Report
National Journal
Congressional Record
Congressional Index

5. For analysis and commentary of bills as they pass through Congress, proceed to:
   CQ Weekly Report
   National Journal
   Washington Post
   New York Times
   Public Affairs Information Service Bulletin

Before compiling an example of a legislative history, it will be useful to summarize the procedures involved in preparing legislative histories. A complete legislative history would include the following:

1. A history of legislative activities and publications, both prior and subsequent to the particular bill. This information is useful in charting changes in social trends and congressional attitudes.
2. A chronological list of how a bill is passed through Congress, including dates, committees, and actions taken.
3. An examination of documents relating to the passage of a bill, including:
   bills

      committee hearings and prints
      committee reports
      debates and proceedings
      presidential messages
      slip law
      veto and congressional action

4. Materials from and recommendations made by executive departments concerning the bill.
5. Materials from and recommendations made by special interest groups participating in the informal legislative process.

Tracing the Privacy Act of 1974

Earlier, the legislative history for the Privacy Act of 1974 was provided, in Table 3. When compiling a legislative history, if the bill number or public law number is known it is fairly easy to find a legislative history already compiled. Each of the tools listed in step 2 of the outline for retrospective tracing provides histories. The legislative history from the 1974 *CIS/ANNUAL* (Part One: "Abstracts of Congressional Publications and Legislative Histories," p. 912) is reprinted in Figure 11. The legislative history taken from the final edition of the *Daily Digest,* January 10, 1975, is reprinted in Figure 12. The *U.S. Code Congressional and Administrative News* for the 93d Congress, 2d session, 1974, contains the legislative history in Figure 13. A similar legislative history also appears in the *U.S. Statutes at Large* (Figure 14), but it is better to use the *U.S. Code Congressional and Administrative News* because it is published much earlier than the *Statutes at Large.* The *Digest of Public General Bills and Resolutions* (93d Congress, 2d session, final issue, pt. 1, pp. 179–80) provides a legislative history in outline form, Figure 15. If the slip law for the Privacy Act of 1974 is available, a legislative history is printed on the inside back cover, Figure 16. Obviously, it is not always possible to find a ready-made legislative history, which is the case if the law has only been passed recently or is still in the legislative process.

Figure 11. *CIS/ANNUAL:* Legislative History

PL93-579   PRIVACY ACT OF 1974.
Dec. 31, 1974.   93-2.   15 p.
*   ●Item 575.
88 STAT. 1896.

"To amend title 5, United States Code, by adding a section 552a to safeguard individual privacy from the misuse of Federal records, to provide that individuals be granted access to records concerning them which are maintained by Federal agencies, to establish a Privacy Protection Study Commission, and for other purposes."

Legislative history: (S. 3418 and related bills):

1970 CIS/Annual:
House Hearings: H621-15.

1972 CIS/Annual:
House Document: H920-1.
Senate Hearings: S521-13; S521-14.

1973 CIS/Annual:
House Hearings: H401-7; H401-9; H401-33.
House Report: H403-11 (No. 93-598).

1974 CIS/Annual:
House Hearings: H401-20; H401-40.
Senate Committee Prints: S402-29; S522-10; S522-12; S522-13; S522-17; S522-18; S522-19; S522-21.
House Report: H403-27 (No. 93-1416, accompanying H.R. 16373).
Senate Report: S403-18 (No. 93-1183).

Congressional Record Vol. 120 (1974):
Nov. 21, considered and passed Senate.
Dec. 11, considered and passed House, amended, in lieu of H.R. 16373.
Dec. 17, Senate concurred in House amendment with amendments.
Dec. 18, House concurred in Senate amendments.

Weekly Compilation of Presidential Documents Vol. 11, No. 1:
Jan. 1, Presidential statement.

Figure 12. *Congressional Record, Daily Digest:* Legislative History

Title	Bill No.	Date introduced	Committee		Date reported		Report No.		Page of Congressional Record of passage		Date of passage		Date approved	Public Law No.
			House	Senate	House	Senate	House	Senate	House	Senate	House	Senate		
To authorize and request the President to call a White House Conference on Library and Information Sciences in 1976.	S.J. Res. 40	Jan. 26 1973	EdL	Com	May 22	Nov. 16 1973	93-1056	93-521	H 11774	S 20847	Dec. 12	Nov. 20 1973	Dec. 31	93-568
To improve veterans' home loan programs.	H.R. 15912 (S. 3883)	July 16 1973	VA	VA	July 29	Dec. 11	93-1213	93-1334	H 7669	S 21396	Aug. 5	Dec. 13	Dec. 31	93-569
Making further continuing appropriations for fiscal year 1975 through Feb. 28, 1975.	H.J. Res.1178	Dec. 17	App	App	Dec. 17	Dec. 18	93-1614	93-1405	H 12226	S 22142	Dec. 18	Dec. 19	Dec. 31	93-570
Providing authority for military bands to make recordings and tapes for commercial sale in connection with the Bicentennial celebration.	H.R. 14401	Apr. 25	AS	AS	Sept. 19	Sept. 12	93-1364	93-1344	H 9950	S 21835	Oct. 7	Dec. 17	Dec. 31	93-571
To provide a program of emergency unemployment compensation for up to an additional 13 weeks.	H.R. 17597	Dec. 10	WM		Dec. 10		93-1549		H 11698	S 21676	Dec. 12	Dec. 16	Dec. 31	93-572
To extend certain copyright laws, and to establish a National Commission on New Technological Uses of Copyrighted Works.	S. 3976	Sept. 9	Jud			Dec. 12	93-1581		H 12360	S 16185	Dec. 19	Sept. 9	Dec. 31	93-573
Granting certain land to the city of Albuquerque for public purposes.	S. 2125	July 9 1973	IIA	IIA	Dec. 13	July 22	93-1592	93-1025	H 12077	S 13391	Dec. 17	July 24	Dec. 31	93-574
Authorizing transfer of certain Colorado lands to the Secretary of Agriculture for purpose of their inclusion in the Arapaho National Forest.	S. 3615	June 10	IIA	IIA	Dec. 13	Aug. 19	93-1596	93-1105	H 12078	S 15407	Dec. 17	Aug. 21	Dec. 31	93-575
Authorizing supplementary funds for the Atomic Energy Commission for fiscal year 1975.	H.R. 16609 (S. 4033)	Sept. 11	AE	AE	Oct. 7	Oct. 8	93-1434	93-1246	H 11015	S 20955	Nov. 25	Dec. 10	Dec. 31	93-576
Providing Federal support for programs of research and development of fuels and energy.	S. 1283	Mar. 19 1973	IIA	IIA	June 26	Dec. 1 1973	93-1157	93-589	H 9139	S 22246	Sept. 11	Dec. 7	Dec. 31	93-577
Authorizing conveyance of certain lands in Yuma County, Ariz., to Wide River Farms, Inc., as a result of change in the course of the Colorado River.	H.R. 13565	June 4	IIA	IIA	Dec. 13	Oct. 10	93-1595	93-1274	H 12078	S 19663	Dec. 17	Nov. 20	Dec. 31	93-578
To protect individual privacy in Federal gathering, use, and disclosure of information.	S. 3418 (H.R. 16373)	May 1	GO	GO	Oct. 2	Sept. 26	93-1416	93-1183	H 11666	S 19858	Dec. 11	Nov. 21	Dec. 31	93-579
Providing for the establishment of an American Indian Policy Review Commission.	S.J. Res. 133 (H.J. Res. 1117)	July 16 1973	IIA	IIA	Oct. 3	Dec. 3 1973	93-1420	93-594	H 10782	S 21879	Nov. 19	Dec. 5 1973	Jan. 2 1975	93-580

Figure 13. *U.S. Code Congressional and Administrative News:* Legislative History

Public Law		88 Stat. Page	Bill No.	Report No. 93–		Comm. Reporting		Cong.Rec.Vol.120 (1974) Dates of Consideration and Passage	
No.93–	Date App.			House	Senate	House	Senate	House	Senate
558	Dec. 30	1793	S. 3191	1544	1229	AS	AS	Dec. 16	Oct. 8
559	Dec. 30	1795	S. 3394	1471	1134	FA	FR	Dec. 11,	Dec. 4,
				1610	1299	Conf	FR	18	17
						(H.R. 17234)			
560	Dec. 30	1820	H.R. 7978	1354	1359	IIA	IIA	Oct. 7	Dec. 16
561	Dec. 30	1821	S.J.Res. 224	none	1294	none	J	Dec. 16	Nov. 21
562	Dec. 30	1821	S. 939	1519	744	IIA	IIA	Dec. 16	Mar. 26
563	Dec. 31	1822	H.R. 16901	1379	1296	App	App	Oct. 9	Nov. 25
				1561		Conf		Dec. 12	Dec. 17
564	Dec. 31	1843	S. 3489	1593	1054	IIA	AgrF	Dec. 17	Aug. 5
565	Dec. 31	1843	S. 3518	1594	1108	IIA	IIA	Dec. 17	Aug. 21
566	Dec. 31	1844	S. 194	1591	679	IIA	IIA	Dec. 17	Feb. 7
567	Dec. 31	1845	H.R. 16596	1528	1327	EL	LPW	Dec. 12,	Dec. 13,
				1621		Conf	(S. 4079)	18	18
568	Dec. 31	1855	S.J.Res. 40	1056	521	EL	C	Dec. 12,	Nov. 20 *
				1619	1409	Conf	Conf	19	Dec. 13, 16, 19
569	Dec. 31	1863	H.R. 15912	1232	1334	VA	VA (S. 3883)	Aug. 5 Dec. 17	Dec. 13
570	Dec. 31	1867	H.J.Res. 1178	1614	1405	App	App	Dec. 18, 19	Dec. 19
571	Dec. 31	1868	H.R. 14401	1364	1344	AS	AS	Oct. 7	Dec. 17
572	Dec. 31	1869	H.R. 17597	1549	none	WM	none	Dec. 12, 19	Dec. 16
573	Dec. 31	1873	S. 3976	1581	none	J	none	Dec. 19	Sept. 9 Dec. 19
574	Dec. 31	1875	S. 2125	1592	1025	IIA	IIA	Dec. 17	July 24
575	Dec. 31	1878	S. 3615	1596	1105	IIA	IIA	Dec. 17	Aug. 21
576	Dec. 31	1878	H.R. 16609	1434	1246	AE	AE (S. 4033)	Nov. 25 Dec. 17	Dec. 10
577	Dec. 31	1878	S. 1283	1157 1563	589	IIA (H.R. 13565) Conf.	IIA	Sept. 11 Dec. 16	Dec. 7 * Dec. 17
578	Dec. 31	1895	S. 3574	1595	1274	IIA	IIA	Dec. 17	Nov. 20
579	Dec. 31	1896	S. 3418	1416	1183	GO (H.R. 16373)	GO	Dec. 11, 18	Nov. 21 Dec. 17, 18

Figure 14. *U.S. Statutes at Large:* Legislative History

A20   GUIDE TO LEGISLATIVE HISTORY OF

No.	Date approved	88 Stat.	Bill No.	Report No.	Committee reporting
	1974				
93–540	Dec. 22	1738	H.R. 6925	93–376	Interior and Insular Affairs
93–541	Dec. 26	1739	S.J. Res. 263		
93–542	Dec. 26	1740	S.J. Res. 234		
93–543	Dec. 26	1740	S. 2343	93–1520	Interior and Insular Affairs
93–544	Dec. 26	1741	H.R. 10834	93–800	Interior and Insular Affairs
93–545	Dec. 26	1741	H.R. 5056	93–1386	Armed Services
93–546	Dec. 26	1742	H.R. 1355	93–1336	Government Operations
93–547	Dec. 26	1742	H.R. 14349	93–1366	Armed Services
93–548	Dec. 26	1743	H.R. 16006	93–1224	Armed Services
93–549	Dec. 26	1743	H.R. 15067	93–1384	Post Office and Civil Service
93–550	Dec. 26	1744	H.R. 11013	93–968	Interior and Insular Affairs
93–551	Dec. 26	1744	H.R. 8864	93–1409	Judiciary
93–552	Dec. 27	1745	H.R. 16136	93–1244	Armed Services
				93–1545	[Conference]
93–553	Dec. 27	1770	S. J. Res. 260		
93–554	Dec. 27	1771	H.R. 16900	93–1378	Appropriations
				93–1503	[Conference]
93–555	Dec. 27	1784	H.R. 7077	93–1511	Interior and Insular Affairs
93–556	Dec. 27	1789	H.R. 16424	93–1395	Government Operations
93–557	Dec. 27	1792	S. 4013	93–1558	Judiciary
93–558	Dec. 30	1793	S. 3191	93–1544	Armed Services
93–559	Dec. 30	1795	S. 3394 (H.R. 17234)	93–1471	Foreign Affairs
				93–1610	[Conference]
93–560	Dec. 30	1820	H.R. 7978	93–1354	Interior and Insular Affairs
93–561	Dec. 30	1821	S.J. Res. 224		
93–562	Dec. 30	1821	S. 939	93–1519	Interior and Insular Affairs
93–563	Dec. 31	1822	H.R. 16901	93–1379	Appropriations
				93–1561	[Conference]
93–564	Dec. 31	1843	S. 3489	93–1593	Interior and Insular Affairs
93–565	Dec. 31	1843	S. 3518	93–1594	Interior and Insular Affairs
93–566	Dec. 31	1844	S. 194	93–1591	Interior and Insular Affairs
93–567	Dec. 31	1845	H.R. 16596 (S. 4079)	93–1528	Education and Labor
				93–1621	[Conference]
93–568	Dec. 31	1855	S.J. Res. 40	93–1056	Education and Labor
				93–1619	[Conference]
93–569	Dec. 31	1863	H.R. 15912 (S. 3883)	93–1232	Veterans' Affairs
93–570	Dec. 31	1867	H.J. Res. 1178	93–1614	Appropriations
93–571	Dec. 31	1868	H.R. 14401	93–1364	Armed Services
93–572	Dec. 31	1869	H.R. 17597	93–1549	Ways and Means
93–573	Dec. 31	1873	S. 3976	93–1581	Judiciary
93–574	Dec. 31	1875	S. 2125	93–1592	Interior and Insular Affairs
93–575	Dec. 31	1878	S. 3615	93–1596	Interior and Insular Affairs
93–576	Dec. 31	1878	H.R. 16609 (S. 4033)	93–1434	Joint Committee on Atomic Energy.
93–577	Dec. 31	1878	S. 1283 (H.R. 13565)	93–1157	Interior and Insular Affairs
				93–1563	[Conference]
93–578	Dec. 31	1895	S. 3574	93–1595	Interior and Insular Affairs
93–579	Dec. 31	1896	S. 3418 (H.R. 16373)	93–1416	Government Operations

Column groups: No. / Date approved / 88 Stat. are under **Public Law**; Report No. / Committee reporting are under **House**. Bill No. stands between.

Senate		Dates of consideration and passage: Congressional Record, Vol. 119 (1973); Vol. 120 (1974)		Presidential statement: Public Papers of the Presidents
Report No.	Committee reporting	House	Senate	
				Ford: 1974
93-1308	Interior and Insular Affairs	Sept. 17, 1973	Dec. 9, 1974	
93-1322	Banking, Housing and Urban Affairs.	Dec. 13, 1974	Dec. 11, 1974	
93-1180	Government Operations	Dec. 17, 1974	Oct. 1, 1974	
93-684	Interior and Insular Affairs	Dec. 16, 1974	Feb. 27, 1974	
93-1186	Interior and Insular Affairs	Feb. 19, Dec. 12, 1974.	Oct. 1, Dec. 14, 1974.	
93-1341	Armed Services	Oct. 7, 1974	Dec. 14, 1974	
93-1329	Government Operations	Oct. 7, 1974	Dec. 12, 1974	
93-1343	Armed Services	Nov. 18, 1974	Dec. 13, 1974	
93-1337	Armed Services	Aug. 5, 1974	Dec. 13, 1974	
93-1339	Post Office and Civil Service	Oct. 7, 1974	Dec. 13, 1974	
93-1221	Interior and Insular Affairs	May 7, Dec. 11, 1974.	Oct. 4, 1974	
93-1352	Judiciary	Nov. 18, 1974	Dec. 16, 1974	
93-1136	Armed Services	Aug. 9, Dec. 12, 1974.	Sept. 11, Dec. 14, 1974.	
93-1255	Appropriations	Dec. 16, 1974 Sept. 30, Oct. 1, 2, Dec. 4, 16, 1974.	Nov. 26, 1974 Oct. 10, Nov. 18-20, Dec. 9-11, 14, 1974.	
93-1328	Interior and Insular Affairs	Dec. 9, 1974	Dec. 12, 1974	Dec. 28.
93-1323	Government Operations	Oct. 7, 1974	Dec. 12, 1974	Dec. 27.
93-1215	Judiciary	Dec. 16, 1974	Oct. 4, 1974	
93-1229	Armed Services	Dec. 16, 1974	Oct. 8, 1974	
93-1134, 93-1299	Foreign Relations	Dec. 10, 11, 18, 1974	Sept. 24, Oct. 1, 2, Dec. 3, 4, 17, 1974.	Dec. 30.
93-1359	Interior and Insular Affairs	Oct. 7, 1974	Dec. 16, 1974	
93-1294	Judiciary	Dec. 16, 1974	Nov. 21, 1974	
93-744	Interior and Insular Affairs	Dec. 16, 1974	Mar. 26, 1974	
93-1296	Appropriations	Oct. 9, Dec. 12, 1974.	Nov. 25, Dec. 17, 1974.	
93-1054	Agriculture and Forestry	Dec. 17, 1974	Aug. 5, 1974	
93-1108	Interior and Insular Affairs	Dec. 17, 1974	Aug. 21, 1974	
93-679	Interior and Insular Affairs	Dec. 17, 1974	Feb. 7, 1974	
93-1327	Labor and Public Welfare	Dec. 12, 18, 1974.	Dec. 13, 18, 1974.	Dec. 31.
93-521	Labor and Public Welfare	Dec. 12, 19, 1974.	Nov. 20, 1973; Dec. 13, 16, 19, 1974.	
93-1409	[Conference]			
93-1334	Veterans' Affairs	Aug. 5, Dec. 17, 1974.	Dec. 12, 13, 1974.	
93-1405	Appropriations	Dec. 18, 19, 1974.	Dec. 19, 1974	
93-1344	Armed Services	Oct. 7, 1974	Dec. 17, 1974	
		Dec. 12, 17, 1974.	Dec. 16, 1974	Dec. 31.
		Dec. 19, 1974	Sept. 9, Dec. 19, 1974.	
93-1025	Interior and Insular Affairs	Dec. 17, 1974	July 24, 1974	
93-1105	Interior and Insular Affairs	Dec. 17, 1974	Aug. 21, 1974	
93-1246	Joint Committee on Atomic Energy.	Nov. 25, Dec. 17, 1974.	Dec. 10, 17, 1974.	
93-589	Interior and Insular Affairs	Aug. 22, Sept. 11, Dec. 16, 1974.	Dec. 5-7, 1973; Dec. 17, 1974.	
				Ford: 1975
93-1274	Interior and Insular Affairs	Dec. 17, 1974	Nov. 20, 1974	
93-1183	Government Operations	Dec. 11, 18, 1974.	Nov. 21, Dec. 17, 1974.	Jan. 1.

Figure 15. *Digest of Public General Bills and Resolutions:* Legislative History

<u>Pub. L. 93-579.</u> Approved 12/31/74: S. 3418.

Privacy Act - Prohibits disclosure by Federal agencies of any record contained in a system of records, except pursuant to a written request by or with the prior written consent of the individual to whom the record pertains. Makes exceptions to this prohibition for use of such records by the individual involved, the Congress, the courts, officers of the agency maintaining the record, the Bureau of the Census, and for criminal and civil law enforcement purposes.

Requires agencies which keep records systems to keep account of disclosures of records, and to inform the subjects of such disclosures.

Allows subjects of records to have access and copying rights to such records. Establishes a procedure for amendment of such records, and of judicial appeal of agency refusal to amend.

Requires relevancy of records to official purposes; accuracy; disclosure of purposes to informants; publication annually of the existence, character, and accessibility of records systems; and appropriate safeguards to maintain confidentiality of such records. Prohibits maintenance of records describing individuals' exercise of first amendment rights, with specified exceptions.

Requires recordkeeping agencies to establish rules relating to notice, access, and amendment.

Permits civil suits against agencies by individuals adversely affected by agency actions not in compliance with this Act. Describes remedies available in such actions.

Sets forth criminal penalties for noncompliance with this Act.

Provides for exemptions from this Act, such as for specified records of the Central Intelligence Agency and records of investigations compiled for law enforcement purposes.

Prohibits an agency from selling or renting an individual's name and address.

Requires agencies to notify the Congress and Office of Management and Budget in advance of any proposal to establish or alter records systems.

Requires the President to report to the Congress annually on the number of records which were exempted from the coverage of this Act.

Establishes the Privacy Protection Study Commission to study government and private data systems and make recommendations for protecting privacy by the application of this Act or additional legislation.

Lists suggestive and required areas of study for the Commission.

Grants subpena power to the Commission.

Makes it unlawful for Federal, State, or local agencies to deny legal rights, benefits, or privileges to individuals because of such individuals' refusal to disclose their social security account number.

5-01-74	Referred to Senate Committee on Government Operations
9-26-74	Reported to Senate, amended, S. Rept. 93-1183
11-21-74	Measure called up by unanimous consent in Senate
11-21-74	Measure considered in Senate
11-21-74	Measure passed Senate, amended, roll call #496 (74-9)
11-22-74	Provisions as passed Senate 11/21/74 inserted in H.R. 16373
12-11-74	Measure called up by unanimous consent in House
12-11-74	Measure considered in House
12-11-74	Measure passed House, amended (provisions of H.R. 16373 inserted as passed House)
12-17-74	Senate agreed to House amendments with an amendment, roll call #567 (77-8)
12-18-74	House agreed to Senate amendments with an amendment
12-18-74	Senate agreed to House amendments to the Senate amendments
12-31-74	Public law 93-579

Figure 16. Slip Law: Legislative History

<u>LEGISLATIVE HISTORY:</u>

HOUSE REPORT No. 93-1416 accompanying H.R. 16373 (Comm. on Government
    Operations).

SENATE REPORT No. 93-1183 (Comm. on Government Operations).
CONGRESSIONAL RECORD, Vol. 120, (1974):
    Nov. 21, considered and passed Senate.
    Dec. 11, considered and passed House, amended, in lieu of
        H.R. 16373
    Dec. 17, Senate concurred in House amendment with amendments.
    Dec. 18, House concurred in Senate amendments.
WEEKLY COMPILATION OF PRESIDENTIAL DOCUMENTS, Vol. 11, No. 1:
    Jan. 1, Presidential statement.

The Privacy Act of 1974 can also be traced through a subject approach. The subject index of the *CIS/ANNUAL,* using the subject heading "Privacy," will also lead the user to Figure 11. Looking under "Privacy" in the index to the *CQ Almanac* would lead the researcher to a three-page synopsis of the Privacy Act *(CQ Almanac,* vol. 30, 1974, pp. 292–94). The index to the *CQ Weekly Report* for 1974 lists eight entries under the heading "Federal Data Banks." One of the entries is to a special report entitled "Privacy: Congress Expected to Vote Controls" *(CQ Weekly Report,* vol. 32, pp. 2611–14). The subject index to *National Journal* (vol. 6, nos. 27–62) has the descriptor "Privacy" as a subheading under "Civil Liberties." That entry refers the researcher to an article entitled "Justice Report/Protection of Citizen's Privacy Becomes Major Federal Concern" *(National Journal,* October 12, 1974, pp. 1521–30). The annual index for the 1975 *U.S. Monthly Catalog* provides seventeen citations to hearings, reports, and other documents under the subject heading "Privacy." The researcher, if interested in prior publications on the topic of privacy, could also check the *Cumulative Subject Index to the Monthly Catalog of United States Government Publications, 1900–1971,* where thirty-five citations are listed under the heading "Privacy." *Public Affairs Information Service Bulletin* (vol. 60, 1973–1974) lists twenty-seven items under "Privacy." Four of those citations are to federal documents, two are articles in *National Journal* and one an article in *CQ Weekly Report.* When conducting a subject search, make a conscious effort to think carefully about all possible appropriate subject headings. Pay close attention to "see" references, for they act as directional signs to other related headings. As shown above, three different subject headings proved fruitful. In a subject approach to legislative tracing you will always get a reference to some document or background article. Once you have tracked down that information, you should have little trouble identifying the bill number or public law number. With either number in hand the tools described earlier can be used to compile a legislative history. All the bibliographic tools used in legislative tracing are always indexed by bill number and/or law number.

Bills take varying lengths of time to pass through Congress; it is unusual for important pieces of legislation to pass in a single year, or even a single Congress. While bills will have different numbers in each Congress, many bills span a great number of years. The historical roots of a bill can sometimes be traced over a prolonged period of years. The Privacy Act of 1974 reflects a long legislative history, extending back to 1965. Between 1965 and 1972, a span of time beginning with the 89th Congress and ending with the 92d, a total of 342 legislative proposals related to privacy were introduced in Congress. Consequently, there is a wealth of government publications about privacy. Since 1965, hundreds of committee hearings and prints and executive publications have been issued. Citing just a few publications will underscore the importance of searching for related documents issued prior to the bill. The President's Commission on Federal Statistics issued in 1971 a two-volume report entitled *Federal Statistics* (Pr37.8:St2/R29), containing chapters entitled "Privacy and Confidentiality," "Statistics and the Problem of Privacy," and "Findings and Recommendations on Privacy and Confidentiality." In July 1973 the Secretary's Advisory Committee on Automated Personal Data Systems of the U.S. Department of Health, Education and Welfare issued a report, *Records, Computers and the Rights of Citizens* (HE1.2:R24/3). A year later the Senate Subcommittee on Constitutional Rights released the six-volume *Federal Data Banks and Constitutional Rights: A Study of Data Systems on Individuals Maintained by Agencies of the United States Government* (Y4.J89/2:C76/20). In addition to a survey of government agencies, the first volume includes informative introductory sections, including "Historical Context" and "Legislative Context." These documents, along with countless others, provide reams of valuable testimony, investigative reports, historical essays, statistics, surveys, recommendations, and findings.

Congress has not completed its work when a bill becomes law. Congress now assumes the responsibility of evaluating the implementation and impact of the law. Every congressional committee is charged with watching over the agencies and programs within its purview. This is a part of the legislative process just as are the activities that lead to a bill's passage. In June 1975 the House Committee on Government Operations published its hearings on the Privacy Act, *Implementation of the Privacy Act of 1974: Data Banks* (Y4.G74/7:P93/5).

The General Accounting Office, often referred to as the

watchdog of Congress, was created in part to assist Congress in fulfilling its oversight responsibilities. The student should always check to see whether the GAO has published a report on the particular area of government operations he is researching. *GAO Review,* a quarterly journal, contains articles on the activities of the General Accounting Office and Congress.

Title VIII of the Congressional Budget Act of 1974 requires the GAO to identify, compile, and disseminate information to Congress for use in fulfilling its oversight and budget monitoring responsibilities. Accordingly, the GAO's Office of Programs publishes yearly the Congressional Sourcebook Series, a set of three volumes:

Requirements for Recurring Reports to the Congress monitors and specifies the requirements for recurring reports to Congress made by all branches of the federal government

Federal Program Evaluations identifies and discusses evaluation reports conducted by or for executive departments, agencies, and federal commissions

Federal Information Sources and Systems identifies and describes information sources and systems on fiscal, budgetary and program data in executive agencies.

Each of the source books is well indexed and is an excellent directory and guide to federal programs and information.

The Congressional Budget Office was established in 1974 as the counterpart to the Office of Management and Budget, whose responsibilities include preparing and administering the budget. The Congressional Budget Office assists Congress by preparing economic forecasts and fiscal policy analyses. The CBO also develops cost estimates for carrying out legislation reported by committees, which can be found in *Staff Working Papers for Congressional Budget Scorekeeping*. This new series adds another dimension to legislative tracing, for it is now possible to ascertain the projected expenditures for any bill or resolution.

Legislative tracing entails searching for documents, both congressional and executive, published after a bill has been signed into law. Seven months after the Privacy Act of 1974 became law, *Privacy, A Public Concern: A Resource Document* (PrEx15.2:P93) was issued under the Office of the President.

The document was based on the proceedings of a seminar on privacy sponsored by the President's Domestic Council Committee on the Right of Privacy and the Council of State Governments. In September 1976 a joint committee print, *Legislative History of the Privacy Act of 1974, S. 3418 (Public Law 93-579)* (Y4.G74/6:L52/3), was issued by the Senate Committee on Government Operations and House Subcommittee on Government Information and Individual Rights. This huge document, almost 1500 pages, recounted the history of the Privacy Act of 1974 and discussed developments since its enactment. In 1977, the Privacy Protection Study Commission, established by the Privacy Act of 1974, issued its first in a series of reports, *Personal Privacy in an Information Society.* As in Table 3, a complete legislative history includes citations to government documents published both prior and subsequent to the passage of a bill through Congress.

After having examined and applied the tools of legislative tracing, the researcher can decide for himself which reference would best fulfill his needs and with which he feels most comfortable. Each tool has advantages; some are more comprehensive, others are published more frequently and quickly. Often the choice of guides depends upon what the researcher is seeking. In some situations, the judgment is dictated by time. When tracing legislation in process, the researcher must use those tools which record the progress of a bill as it occurs. Speed and frequency of publication qualify the *Congressional Monitor, Congressional Index, CQ Weekly Report, National Journal, Calendars of House and History of Legislation, CIS/INDEX,* and the *Congressional Record* as the tools best suited for current legislative tracing.

Researching Legislators

The legislative process is more complex than the formal procedures by which a bill becomes law. When we read in the news and hear on television what Congress does, we must realize that Congress is composed of 535 individuals. Congress is not an entity that acts as a single harmonious body, but is composed of men and women with multifarious philosophies and views. The legislative process is the working of individuals and coalitions. To understand how Congress works it is necessary to know something about the members of Congress, for it is the individual representatives and senators who introduce bills, work on committees, and vote on bills. If we look even closer, we see that the legislative process encompasses a vast web of people, including staff members, researchers, lawyers, and lobbyists. This section is intended to introduce the researcher to some of the basic reference works relating to Congress. When actually tracing legislation or researching a legislator, the researcher will need to use additional sources, such as newspapers, periodicals, and scholarly works.

Directories

Directories are vital reference tools when you are making an inquiry about a legislator. Often the researcher needs to find the legislator's address, which committees he serves on, or some biographical information. The following list of annotated references gives an indication of the kinds of information various directories provide.

> U.S. Congress. *Biographical Directory of the American Congress, 1774–1971.* Rev. ed. Washington, D.C.: G.P.O., 1972.
>
> Provides short biographies, arranged alphabetically, of senators and representatives who served in Congress from 1774–1971. Also included is a chronological list of executive officers of administrations from 1789–1971, a list of delegates to the Continental Congress, and a list of Congresses by date and session. There is also a companion volume which covers the lives of people who have served in the executive branch: *Biographic Directory of the United States Executive Branch, 1774–1977,* edited by Robert Sobel.

> U.S. Congress. *Congressional Directory.* Washington, D.C.: G.P.O., 1809–.
>
> Published annually, this directory contains biographical, organizational, and statistical information about members and administrative units of the government. The *Directory* is a who's who of the Congress and all government departments. The *Directory* includes: (1) biographical sketches of legislators, (2) state delegations, (3) terms of service, (4) committees, (5) congressional sessions, (6) governors of states, (7) votes cast for legislators, (8) biographical sketches of Cabinet members and Supreme Court Justices, (9) officials of independent agencies, (10) press galleries, (11) maps of congressional districts and (12) an index of individuals. Material about individual members is submitted by the members themselves. In 1978, a supplement to the *Directory* was issued; this was the first time a supplement has appeared between printings of the complete *Directory.*

Congressional Staff Directory. Compiled and edited by Charles B. Brownson. Alexandria, Va.: Congressional Staff Directory, 1959–.

This yearly publication is a companion to the official *Congressional Directory.* It lists the staffs of all legislators, the committees and subcommittees of both houses, and short biographical sketches of key staff personnel. Included are the committee and subcommittee assignments, key federal officials and their liaison staffs, and an index of personal names. An alphabetical list of cities with population of over 1500 provides the latest census figures, number of the congressional district, and the names of the legislators. Prior to the publication of the *Congressional Staff Directory* every April, a *C.S.D. Advance Locator* is issued at the beginning of the year. The *C.S.D. Advance Locator* helps to fill the information gap until the complete *Directory* is published. Before each congressional election, an advance *C.S.D. Election Index* is published, in September, previewing candidates, providing past election statistics, and listing the cities and towns in each district.

Barone, Michael; Grant Ujifos; and Douglas Matthews; eds. *The Almanac of American Politics: The Senators, the Representatives—Their Records, States and Districts.* Boston: Gambit, 1972–.

An extensive guide to legislators and their districts. Background material contained within this volume is invaluable. The work is arranged alphabetically by state. An introductory description of the state's political background precedes a section covering legislators, giving sketches of their backgrounds, ideology, and record. More important, it provides short outlines of their careers, the committees they serve on, their record on key votes, and their electoral history. Also included are ratings on legislators by interest groups, such as the AFL-CIO's Committee on Political Education (which rates members of Congress on their voting related to labor issues). Finally, there is a profile of each district within the state. Included in this section is the political background of the district, census data, federal outlays, tax burdens, and characteristics of the voters. The work is biennially revised and updated.

Who's Who in American Politics: A Biographical Directory of United States Political Leaders. New York: R. R. Bowker, 1967–.

63

Presents biographical data about 12,500 political figures, from the President to local leaders, including federal government employees, national party leaders, state legislators, local officials of large cities, country chairmen of parties, and minority party leaders. Information includes address, party affiliation, education, family data, political and business background, and achievements. The directory is revised biennially.

Who's Who in Government. Indianapolis: Marquis Who's Who, 1972–.

Provides biographical information on political leaders at the federal and state level. Basically, this work presents the same information as *Who's Who in American Politics.* Its value lies in the format of its indexes. One index arranges political figures according to office within the government structure; a second arranges politicians according to type of responsibilities.

National Roster of Black Elected Officials. Washington, D.C.: Joint Center for Political Studies, 1969–.

This annual work lists black elected officials at all levels of government and provides the mailing address and office held; it also provides an analysis of changes by region, state, and level of office. The Joint Center also publishes a monthly newsletter entitled *Focus,* which regularly contains articles concerning congressional affairs affecting blacks.

Christopher, Maurine. *Black Americans in Congress.* Rev. ed. New York: Thomas Y. Crowell, 1976.

Contains biographical essays of past and contemporary black American legislators. The book spans the period from 1870 to 1970 and has sketches on forty-six individuals. The work has a chronological list of members of Congress, an extensive bibliography, and a subject index.

Engelbarts, Rudolf. *Women in the United States Congress, 1917–1972: Their Accomplishments; with Bibliographies.* Littleton, Colo.: Libraries Unlimited, 1974.

The best reference work on women in Congress, the book has a lengthy introductory essay on the history and role of women in Congress. Descriptive information on congresswomen is listed in chronological order, and arranged in two lists, one for the House of Representatives and the other for the Senate. Each biographical entry includes party affiliation, state elected from, period of service, précis of congressional career, and a bibliography. There is a bibliography on subjects related to the study of women and politics. The work is indexed by individual's name and subject. For current information about women in Congress, the National Women's Political Caucus publishes a newsletter and *Women's Political Times*. There are two other guides to women in Congress which can be used to supplement the Engelbarts volume:

Tolchin, Susan. *Women in Congress: 1917–1976.* Washington, D.C.: G.P.O., 1976.

Chamberlin, Hope. *A Minority of Members: Women in the U.S. Congress.* New York: Praeger, 1973.

Center for the American Woman and Politics. *Women in Public Office: A Biographical Directory and Statistical Analysis.* New York: R. R. Bowker, 1976.

A comprehensive directory of women in public office at all levels of government.

Ralph Nader Congress Project. *Citizens Look at Congress.* Washington, D.C.: Grossman Publishers, 1972–1976.

This series provides detailed profiles, including biographies, voting records, interest group ratings, and the personal financial and legislative interests of legislators elected in the 1972 election. Much of the information was gathered through personal interviews and is not always reliable. The set has the distinction of being interesting and lively reading. The Congress Project has started to publish similar works focusing on House and Senate committees, revenue committees, commerce committees, environmental committees, and money committees. *Ruling Congress: A Study of How the House and Senate Rules Govern the Legislative Process* (Grossman Publishers), also by the Congress Project, relates directly to legislative tracing.

Directory of Registered Lobbyists and Lobbyist Legislation. 2d ed. Chicago: Marquis Academic Media, 1976.

A comprehensive source book of all registered lobbyists in Washington and the forty-eight states requiring registration. Arranged by state, with lobbyists listed alphabetically. Name, address, phone number, and organizational ties are given for each lobbyist. For easy reference use, there is a lobbyist index and organization index. The com- **65** plete texts of all federal and state laws relating to lobbying are reprinted.

The Washington Influence Directory. Edited by Ed Zuckerman and Amelia Zuckerman. Washington, D.C.: Amward Publications, 1975.

This directory lists lobbyists in an alphabetical name index and cross-indexes them according to their business or organizational affiliation. A third part of the guide indexes the political action committees of corporations, unions, and professional associations.

Taylor's Encyclopedia of Government Officials: Federal and State. Dallas: Political Research, 1969–.

This work is not really an encyclopedia, but a directory of members of the federal and state government departments and agencies. No biographical information is given for officials; the value of this series is its quarterly supplements, listing changes, additions, and corrections. Thus the series records changes far in advance of the annual directories.

Telephone Directory: United States Senate. Washington, D.C.: G.P.O., 1978–.

Telephone Directory: United States House of Representatives. Washington, D.C.: G.P.O., 1978–.

These two directories provide a name and location list of all House and Senate employees, including members, their Washington and field office staffs, committee and subcommittee members and staff, and support office staff.

Goldman, Perry, and James S. Young, eds. *The United States Congressional Directories, 1789–1840.* New York: Columbia University Press, 1973.

U.S. Congress. Joint Committee on Printing. *Congressional Pictorial Directory.* Washington, D.C.: G.P.O., 1951–. [Annual.]

Leaders in Profile: The United States Senate. New York: Sperr and Douth, 1972–. [Editions for each Congress.]

Morris, Dan, and Inez Morris. *Who Was Who in American Politics: A Biographical Dictionary of Over 4,000 Men and Women Who Contributed to the United States Political Scene from the Colonial Days Up to and including the Immediate Past.* New York: Hawthorn Books, 1974.

Congressional Yellow Book: A Loose-leaf Directory of Members of Congress, Their Committees, and Key Aides. Edited by Michaela Buhler and Dorothy Lee Jackson. Washington: Washington Monitor, 1977–.

The Federal Telephone Directory. Washington, D.C.: Consolidated Directories, 1974–.

Election Statistics

Collecting and disseminating statistics is a meticulous and time-consuming activity which all modern nations undertake. Census data and economic indicators are the first statistical measures governments systematically collect. Historically, the need for gathering election statistics has been a recent phenomenon. In the United States, the evolution of systematically recording election statistics has been intertwined with the political process itself. A quintessential element of the democratic process is the documentation and distribution of electoral statistics. The availability of election data makes it theoretically possible for every citizen to scrutinize and question campaign practices and outcomes. A recent landmark in the collection of election statistics was the Federal Election Campaign Act of 1971, which requires the federal government to publish and provide public access to information concerning campaign contributions to candidates running for federal office.

Election statistics are important to the citizen or scholar who is interested in analyzing the ideological or philosophical justifications of the electoral system. For this kind of statistical inspection, the scholar requires data which permit comparability over long periods of time. Two factors also allow for more convenient examination of election statistics. The greater the breakdown of tabulations, the more useful the data will be to the researcher. Second, to engage in a rigorous study of elections the scholar needs to check his data against several sources.

Congressional Quarterly. *Guide to U.S. Elections.* Washington, D.C.: Congressional Quarterly, 1975.

This is the most definitive source of statistical data on congressional elections. Included are the complete voting records of elections for the presidency, Congress, and governorships. This volume is an excellent reference guide to all aspects of elections, because of the extensive background material on the history of political parties, convention ballots and platforms, preference primaries, demographic data, the electoral college, and redistricting and because a topical bibliography accompanies each major section of the work.

The format makes this an especially useful reference work. There are three ways to locate information. A detailed table of contents provides an overview of the scope and coverage of the work; use it for quick and easy access to major sections. There are Candidate Indexes for presidential, gubernatorial, Senate, and House candidates; use these to pinpoint voting returns for over 60,000 candidates. A general index covers all subjects. Congressional Quarterly has published a supplement to the *Guide to U.S. Elections* entitled *Guide to 1976 Elections.*

Congressional Quarterly also publishes the official presidential and congressional election results in the *CQ Weekly Reports.* Here are some special *CQ Reports* on presidential election year results:

CQ Weekly Report, Special Supplement to May 10, 1957, Weekly Report. What Happened in the 1956 Elections: A Congressional District Analysis of the Official 1956 Vote for President, Senator and Representative.

CQ Weekly Report, Special Supplement to March 20, 1959, Weekly Report. What Happened in the 1958 Elections: A Congressional District Analysis of the Official 1958 Vote for Governor, Senator, Representative.

CQ Special Report, Part II of CQ Weekly Report No. 10, March 10, 1961. Complete Returns of the 1960 Elections by Congressional District: A State and District Analysis of the Official 1960 Vote for President, Governor, Senator, Representative.

CQ Special Report, Part I of CQ Weekly Report No. 14, April 5, 1963. Complete Returns of the 1962 Elections by Congressional District: A State and District

Analysis of the Official 1962 Vote for Governor, Senator, Representative.

CQ Special Report, Part I of CQ Weekly Report No. 13, March 26, 1965. Complete Returns of the 1964 Elections by Congressional District: A State and District Breakdown of the Official Vote for President, Governor, Senator, and Representative.

CQ Weekly Report, Special Report Part I of Report No. 19, May 12, 1967. Complete Returns of the 1966 Elections by Congressional Districts: A State and District Analysis of the Official 1966 Vote for Governors, Senators, and Representatives.

CQ Weekly Report Supplement, Part I of CQ Weekly Report No. 23, June 6, 1969. Complete Returns of the 1968 Elections by Congressional District.

CQ Weekly Report No. 46, Nov. 6, 1970. The 1970 Election Results and Analysis.

CQ Weekly Report Supplement to No. 8, Feb. 23, 1974. Complete 1972 Vote by State, Congressional District.

CQ Weekly Report No. 8, February 23, 1974. The 1974 Elections: Pre-primary Campaign Reports, Final 72 Returns, by District.

Congressional Quarterly also publishes the unofficial election results in the *Weekly Report* the week following the election. The results of the 1976 elections (November 2, 1976), for example, were published in the November 6 issue of *CQ Weekly Report* (no. 45).

Cox, Edward Franklin. *State and National Voting in Federal Elections, 1910–1970.* Hamden, Conn.: Archon Books, 1972.

This work uses the national elective format for its data. Tables are by nation and state, including the total vote and percentages of all votes. Voting information covers presidential and congressional elections. Data on the election of representatives is compiled on a statewide aggregate basis. Election data for representatives is not broken down by congressional district, which is a serious drawback. The national elective format provides a useful method for comparing the vote of the three national elective positions. With this kind of format it is simple to measure the voting strength of each party for President, senators, and representatives in each election. The compendium suffers from poor layout, making interpretation of the tables difficult and tedious.

69

Government Affairs Institute [Washington, D.C.].
*America Votes: A Handbook of Contemporary American
Election Statistics.* Compiled and edited by Richard M.
Scammon. New York: Macmillan, 1955–. [Biennial.]

This work includes presidential, congressional, and
gubernatorial returns. The total vote (Republican and
Democratic), pluralities, and percentages per county and
congressional district are reported. Sections on each of the
states include (1) a profile of the state, giving the population, electoral vote, incumbent senators, representatives,
and governors, composition of the state legislature by
party, and the postwar vote for governor and senator; (2) a
map of the state, depicting counties and congressional
districts; (3) a geographical breakdown by county and districts for presidential, senatorial, and gubernatorial returns; and (4) tables of the congressional returns. Every
volume is virtually an almanac for each election year.

U.S. Congress. House. Clerk of the House of Representatives. *Statistics of the Presidential and Congressional
Elections.* Washington, D.C.: G.P.O., 1920–.

The official account of election returns for congressional
and presidential elections, this publication began with the
November 2, 1920, election. The series lacks any geographical breakdown of election returns. It has no real
reference value, but is of interest as the official government record.

Statistical Abstract of the United States. Washington,
D.C.: U.S. Bureau of the Census, Department of Commerce, 1878–.

This annual document is the basic statistical abstract
for data on social, economic, and political affairs in the
United States. Dating back to 1878, the coverage on elections varies considerably over the years. Recent volumes
include information on votes cast in presidential, congressional, and gubernatorial elections, voter registration and
participation, voting-age population, and campaign expenditures. The work is useful for locating other sources of
data through its bibliographic citations. The series includes a wealth of additional background information
which can be used in conjunction with the study of elections. There are statistics on education, employment, income, housing, communication, etc. As a general statistical compendium, the series is recognized by scholars and

researchers alike as a standard source of data on almost every aspect of society. For retrospective coverage of colonial times, volumes of the *Statistical Abstract* should be used in conjunction with the *Historical Statistics of the United States, Colonial Times to 1970, Bicentennial Edition.* Washington, D.C.: Bureau of the Census, Department of Commerce, 1975.

There are individual compilations of congressional election statistics for almost every state. These compendia are published by state historical societies, legislative research bureaus, and university institutes. An example is *Minnesota Votes: Election Returns by County for Presidents, Senators, Congressmen, and Governors, 1857–1977* (St. Paul: Minnesota Historical Society, 1977).

BIBLIOGRAPHIES ON ELECTIONS

Bone, Hugh A. "American Party Politics, Elections, and Voting Behavior," *Annals of the American Academy of Political and Social Science* 372 (1967): 124–37.
Bone, Hugh A. "Selected Bibliography in American Parties and Elections, 1967–1971: A Brief Annotation," *Annals of the American Academy of Political and Social Science* 402 (1972): 117–31.
These two excellent review articles are concerned with the major literature on parties, elections, and voting behavior. Together the two articles cover the period from 1961 to 1971. Both reviews cover only books and monographs, including texts, general works, historical and new theoretical works. The two essays are especially useful for identifying major works and new trends of thought in electoral politics.

Wynar, Lubomyr R., comp. *American Political Parties: A Selective Guide to Parties and Movements of the 20th Century.* Littleton, Colo.: Libraries Unlimited, 1969.
An uneven compilation of over 3,000 books, monographs, and dissertations on significant twentieth-century American parties and movements. Arrangement is by subject and party. The book is helpful in providing general background material related to elections, public opinion, parties, and political behavior.

Agranoff, Robert. *Elections and Electoral Behavior: A Bibliography.* De Kalb: Center for Governmental Studies, Northern Illinois University, 1972.

71

A listing of over three hundred items dealing with theoretical and practical issues of elections. The bibliography is divided into four sections: (1) electoral systems and voting rights; (2) candidate selection, nominations, party conventions; (3) voting behavior; and (4) electoral interpretation. Entries are not annotated, nor is the pagination given for either articles or books.

Smith, Dwight L., and Lloyd W. Garrison, eds. *The American Political Process: Selected Abstracts of Periodical Literature (1954–1971)*. Santa Barbara: ABC-Clio, 1972.
This work contains a lengthy section on American elections, including a subsection on congressional elections and campaigns. The abstracts in the work were taken from *Historial Abstracts* and *America: History and Life*.

Data Archives

There are many data archives throughout the country with holdings which include quantitative data on congressional elections. The major social science data archive is the Inter-University Consortium for Political Research (ICPR) at the University of Michigan. One among the many major files of data available from ICPR is *Historical Election Returns, 1824–1972*. This collection of election data contains county-level returns for presidential, gubernatorial, and congressional elections. Another useful file is the *Congressional Roll Call Records,* which includes the complete roll-call records for both chambers of Congress from 1787 to 1972. For more information about the archive's holdings, consult the ICPR *Guide to Resources and Services, 1977–1978* (Ann Arbor: University of Michigan, 1977).

In addition to the election data cited above, the ICPR holds many other interesting data files on congressional elections. There are some files on specific preference primaries and elections in particular states. Many of the statistical sources mentioned earlier in the guide, such as Census Bureau publications, are available on tape. For example, the *Congressional District Data Book* and *County and City Data Books* are available. Here is a selected list of ICPR data holdings:

Commission on the Operation of the Senate. *Daily Operation of the United States Senate, 1975.*

Lazarsfeld, Paul F.; Bernard R. Berelson; and William N. McPhee. *1948 Elmira Study.*

Lazarsfeld, Paul F.; Bernard R. Berelson; and Hazel Gandet. *1940 Erie County Study.*

O'Leary, Michael; David Kovenock; and Roger Davidson. *Congressional Attitudes towards Congressional Organization.*

McKibben, Carroll L. *Biographical Characteristics of the United States Congress, 1789–1977.*

Miller, Warren E., and Donald E. Stokes. *1958 American Representation Study.*

National Opinion Research Center. *1944 National Election Study.*

National Opinion Research Center. *1948 National Election Study.*

United Nations Association of the United States of America. *1975 Congressional Survey.*

Survey Research Center. *SRC 1948 American National Election Study.*

Survey Research Center. *SRC 1952 American National Election Study.*

Survey Research Center. *SRC 1956 American National Election Study.*

Survey Research Center. *SRC 1958 American National Election Study.*

Survey Research Center. *SRC 1960 American National Election Study.*

Survey Research Center. *SRC 1960 Minor American Election Study.*

Survey Research Center. *SRC 1962 American National Election Study.*

Survey Research Center. *SRC 1964 American National Election Study.*

Survey Research Center. *SRC 1966 American National Election Study.*

Survey Research Center. *SRC 1968 American National Election Study.*

Center for Political Studies. *CPS 1970 American National Election Study.*

Center for Political Studies. *CPS 1972 American National Election Study.*

Center for Political Studies. *CPS 1974 American National Election Study.*

Center for Political Studies. *CPS 1976 American National Election Study.*

Survey Research Center. *American Election Panel Study: 1956, 1958, 1960.*

Survey Research Center. *SRC Domestic Affairs Study, October, 1954.*

ICPSR. *Historical Election Returns, 1788–1976.*

ICPSR. *Candidate Name and Constituency Totals, 1824–1972.*

ICPSR. *Congressional Rosters.*

ICPSR. *Roster of Congressional Officeholders, 1789–1977.*

ICPSR. *United States Congressional Roll Call Voting Records, 1789–1976.*

ICPSR. *Referenda and Primary Election Materials.*

There are a number of other institutions which also have data archives with files on congressional elections and activities. To locate other institutions and their holdings, consult the following sources:

Sessions, Vivian S., ed. *Directory of Data Bases in the Social and Behavioral Sciences.* New York: Science Associates/International, 1974.

An extensive listing of 685 data bases and centers in the United States. For each data base, the following information is provided: (1) address, (2) director and principal staff, (3) data holdings, (4) storage media, and (5) avenue of access. Over fifteen institutions are identified that have data holdings relating to election returns and electoral behavior. The work is also well indexed; included are a subject index, institutional index, and geographical index. The subject index contains several relevant entries: election data, election returns, election studies, electoral data, and electoral studies.

SS Data: Newsletter of Social Science Archival Acquisitions 1, no. 1 (Sept. 1971).

This newsletter is published quarterly by the Laboratory for Political Research of the University of Iowa. The *Newsletter* provides information on data acquired by archives throughout the United States and Canada. The data set descriptions are provided by the participating archives. The descriptions usually include: (1) the original data collection agency and principal investigator and (2) the time period of the data, the population, and a descriptive paragraph explaining the nature of the study.

Party Strength

Voting returns by themselves do not convey the entire story of an election. Students can learn considerably more about elections by developing their own statistical measures. Today, political scientists are employing statistical data in highly sophisticated computations. By using data in different configurations, the researcher can bring to light new perspectives on elections. The following works are the major studies which have sought to examine concepts of party strength, competitiveness, and voting behavior.

Cox, Edward Franklin. *Voting in Postwar Federal Elections: A Statistical Analysis of Party Strengths since 1945.* Rev. ed. Dayton, Ohio: Wright State University, 1968.

As an interpretation of the significance of American voting in federal elections from 1946 to 1966, the book presents measures of party performance, strength, competitiveness, and individual candidate performance. Geographical analyses are by district and state. The author delineates major trends for party competition. The book includes two chapters on the methods of statistical analysis employed in the study. The analyses of the eleven federal elections examined are presented in 251 tables. One failing is the lack of an index.

Cummings, Milton C., Jr. *Congressmen and the Electorate: Elections for the U.S. House and President, 1920–1964.* New York: Free Press, 1966.

An extensive analysis of the interrelationships between for representatives and President in presidential election years. The central thrust of the book is its examination of the similarities and differences between presidential and congressional support polled by the major parties. Other issues covered in the book are ticket-splitting, party strength, the role of minor parties, and the impact of the electoral system on presidential and congressional elections. Includes fifty-one statistical tables relating to the topics discussed.

David, Paul T. *Party Strength in the United States, 1872–1970.* Charlottesville: University Press of Virginia, 1972.

Provides index numbers for party strength for the period from 1872 to 1970. The study contains the percentages of the vote won by Democratic, Republican, and other parties and candidates in presidential, gubernatorial, and congressional elections; it provides statistical and technical background to the formulation of the index numbers. Additional data covering the 1972 elections can be found in:

David, Paul T. "Party Strength in the United States: Changes in 1972." *Journal of Politics* 36, no. 3 (Aug. 1974): 785–96.

David, Paul T. "Party Strength in the United States: Some Corrections." *Journal of Politics* 37, no. 4 (May 1975): 641–42.

David, Paul T. "Party Strength in the United States: Changes in 1976." *Journal of Politics* 40, no. 3 (Aug. 1978): 770–80.

Voter Characteristics

When studying elections it is crucial to know something about the voters. Factors such as age, sex, race, education, and income can help explain why the electorate voted a certain way. On an individual basis, this kind of information is generally available only from public opinion surveys. The largest producer of aggregate data is the U.S. Bureau of the Census. Virtually hundreds of political, economic, and social variables can be drawn from census data. There are data on hundreds of subject categories and they are often broken down geographically by congressional districts, counties, standard metropolitan statistical areas, unincorporated places, and city blocks.

With some patience the researcher can find what he is seeking.

U.S. Bureau of the Census. *Congressional District Data Book, 93d Congress: A Statistical Abstract Supplement.* Washington, D.C.: G.P.O., 1973.

The *Congressional District Data Book* presents a wide range of data from the 1970 census, and recent election statistics for districts of the 93d Congress, elected in 1972. Socioeconomic data, such as population, sex, residency, race, age, households and families, marital status, industry, occupation, migration, and housing, are reported. Maps for each state show counties and congressional districts. Appendixes give data on apportionment, redistricting, and the population of the districts of the 88th and 93d Congresses. This is the third *CDDB*. Previous editions were published for the 87th Congress (1960) and the 88th Congress (1962). The second *CDDB* was updated by a series of supplements for states redistricted for the 88th and 90th Congresses. The *Congressional District Data Book* for the 94th Congress was to be issued in the spring of 1977, but has not yet been published. Congressional Quarterly has published a condensed version of the *Congessional District Data Book, Congressional Districts in the 1970's* (2d ed., 1974), which contains the essential demographic and political information on all 435 congressional districts. While the Congressional Quarterly volume is not as encompassing as the Census series, it is easier and quicker to use.

U.S. Bureau of the Census. *County and City Data Book: A Statistical Abstract Supplement.* Washington, D.C.: G.P.O., 1977.

The ninth in a series dating back to 1947, this work presents a wide range of statistical information for counties, standard metropolitan statistical areas, cities, urbanized areas, and unincorporated places. Included are data on agriculture, bank deposits, birth and death rates, business firms, crime, education, employment, governmental revenue and expenditures, housing, income, migration, public assistance, savings, social security, and presidential voting.

The U.S. Census Bureau publishes two series within their Current Population Reports that provide information on various aspects of the voting population. The *Population Estimates, P-25 Series* includes regular reports on the estimates and projections of population by voting age. The *Population Characteristics, P-20 Series* provides information about the demographic characteristics of the voting population and the degree of participation in general elections by those eligible to vote. Those reports, as well as others published by the Census Bureau, are indexed in the *Bureau of the Census Catalog* (1790–) and the *American Statistics Index: A Comprehensive Guide and Index to the Statistical Publications of the U.S. Government* (Washington, D.C.: Congressional Information Service, 1973–).

The *American Statistics Index* is the most inclusive index to statistics published by the federal government. Like *CIS/INDEX*, the *American Statistics Index* provides abstracts of the documents it indexes. The index covers the publications of all major statistical agencies and statistics reported in committee hearings and prints. Without this index, it would be impossible to systematically search for statistics published in hearings and prints. The American Political Science Association has published two guides to census data in its Instructional Monograph Series: *U.S. Census Data for Political and Social Research: A Manual for Students* and *A Resource Guide* (1976). Both were prepared by Phyllis G. Carter, formerly chief of the Census History Staff, Data User Services Division of the Bureau of the Census.

> *Population Estimates, P-25 Series.*
> *Estimates of the Population of Voting Age, by States: 1948.* No. 15, Oct. 10, 1948.
> *Estimates of the Population of the United States and Components of Population Change: 1950–1954.* No. 90, March 7, 1954.
> *Estimates of the Civilian Population of Voting Age, for States.* No. 143, Nov. 1952 and 1956, Oct. 5, 1956.
> *Estimates of the Civilian Population of Voting Age, for States.* No. 185, Nov. 1958, Oct. 22, 1960.
> *Estimates of the Civilian Population of Voting Age, for States.* No. 221, Nov. 1960, Oct. 7, 1960.
> *Estimates of the Civilian Population of Voting Age, for States.* No. 225, Nov. 1962, Oct. 12, 1962.
> *Estimates of the Population of Voting in General Elections, 1920–1964.* No. 315, Aug. 19, 1965.
> *Projections of the Population of Voting Age: Nov. 1966 and 1968.* No. 325, Jan. 25, 1966.

Projections of the Population of Voting Age, for States: Nov. 1966 and 1968. No. 342, June 27, 1966.

Estimates of the Population of Voting Age, for States: Nov. 1, 1968. No. 406, Oct. 4, 1968.

Projections of the Population of Voting Age, for States: Nov. 1972. No. 479, March 1972.

Projections of the Population of Voting Age, for States: Nov. 1974. No. 526, Sept. 1974.

Projections of the Population of Voting Age, for States: November 1976. No. 626, May 1976.

Language Minority, Illiteracy, and Voting Data Used in Making Determinations for the Voting Rights Act Amendments of 1975 (Public Law 94-73). No. 627, June 1976.

Population Characteristics, P-20 Series.

Voter Participation in the National Election, Nov. 1964. No. 143, Oct. 25, 1965.

Characteristics of Persons of Voting Age, 1964–1968. No. 172, May 3, 1968.

Voting and Registration in the Election of Nov. 1966. No. 174, Aug. 8, 1968.

Voter Participation in Nov. 1968. No. 177, Dec. 27, 1968.

Voting and Registration in the Election of Nov. 1968. No. 192, Dec. 2, 1969.

Voter Participation in Nov. 1970. No. 208, Dec. 24, 1970.

Characteristics of New Voters: 1972. No. 230, Dec. 1971.

Voter Participation in Nov. 1972. No. 244, Dec. 1972.

Voting and Registration in the Election of Nov. 1972. No. 253, Oct. 1973.

Voter Participation in Nov. 1974. No. 275, Jan. 1975.

Voting and Registration in the Election of November 1974. No. 293, April 1976.

Voter Participation in November 1976. No. 304, Dec. 1976. [Advance report.]

Campaign Finances

One badly neglected area of election statistics is campaign contributions. Only since 1972 has a systematic collection of data on campaign contributions been undertaken. As the issue of money in elections has always been prominent, the massive volumes of campaign contribution statistics should lead to many new and fascinating studies. At present, the most valuable and inclusive source on political contributors is published by the federal government. In accordance with the Federal Election Campaign Act of 1971 (Public Law 92–225), the General Accounting Office, Clerk of the House, and the Secretary of the Senate are responsible for making public statistics on contributions to presidential and congressional candidates.

Beginning with the 1972 elections, it is now possible to do extensive research on campaign expenditures. The materials issued by Common Cause and the federal government provide bounteous data on campaign spending. By using both sources of information, one can examine campaign spending according to: (1) candidate, (2) party, (3) contest, (4) committee, (5) type of contribution, (6) size of contribution, and (7) state. The amount of statistics now published provides researchers with considerable raw data for extended analyses. With the continuation of those publications, researchers will also have the opportunity to conduct time-series studies. For information on the historical background of the Federal Election Campaign Act of 1971, consult the first two publications listed below.

> U.S. Congress. Senate. Select Committee on Presidential Activities. *Electoral Reform: Basic References.* Committee print pursuant to S. Res. 60, 93d Cong., 1st Sess., 1973.
>
> The main body of this work is a collection of eighteen essays and reports on the issue of campaign spending. The articles have been well chosen and provide a good discussion of the issue. The work includes a short history of the major events in the movement for federal campaign reform. There is an annotated bibliography of selected references on financing political campaigns. The bibliography covers 1967 to 1973. The text of the Federal Election Campaign Act of 1971 is reprinted.

> U.S. Congress. Senate. Committee on Rules and Administration. Subcommittee on Privileges and Elections. *Federal Election Campaign Laws.* Washington, D.C.: G.P.O., 1975.
>
> A compilation of all federal laws affecting federal elections and campaign practices. Included are the Federal Election Campaign Act of 1971, the Federal Election Act

Amendments of 1974, and the Hatch Act. These laws, as
well as commentaries on them, can also be found reprinted
in various Congressional Quarterly publications.

Agranoff, Robert. *Political Campaigns: A Bibliography.*
De Kalb: Center for Governmental Studies, Northern
Illinois University, 1972.
A bibliography of about two hundred unannotated citations. The bibliography is general, focusing on three
areas: (1) campaign strategies, electioneering, and party
activities, (2) campaign techniques, media advertising,
polls, and (3) campaigns and election finance.

U.S. Congress. Senate. *Factual Campaign Information.*
Compiled by the Senate Library under the direction of
the Secretary of the Senate. Washington, D.C.: G.P.O.,
1939–.
This series is compiled to serve senators in their campaigns. It contains limited statistical data, with the accent
on senatorial elections, but includes information about
minor parties and presidential and congressional
primaries. A lengthy section covers the major statutory
provisions governing federal elections as well as other
miscellaneous laws. Another section deals with party organization, both Republican and Democratic. Members of
national committees, senatorial campaign committees,
and national congressional committees, and chairmen of
state committees are listed.

Citizens' Research Foundation. *CRF Listing of Contributors of National Level Political Committees to Incumbents and Candidates for Public Office.* Edited by
Herbert E. Alexander and Caroline D. Jones. Princeton,
N. J.: Citizens' Research Foundation, 1968–1970.
Provides data on contributions given to candidates by
national-level political committees of the Republican and
Democratic parties, as well as committees representing
labor, business, and professional interests.

Citizens' Research Foundation. *CRF Listing of Political
Contributors of $500 or More.* Edited by Herbert E.
Alexander and Caroline D. Jones. Princeton, N.J.: Citi-
zens' Research Foundation, 1968–1972.
A listing of contributors, arranged alphabetically, who
gave to candidates at both the national and state level.

The address of the contributor, the amount of the contribution, the candidate, and party to which it was given are provided.

Citizens' Research Foundation. *CRF Listing of Contributors and Lenders of $10,000 or More in 1972.* Edited by Barbara D. Paul, Mary Jo Long, Elizabeth C. Burns, and Herbert Alexander. Princeton, N.J.: Citizens' Research Foundation, 1975.

A compilation of campaign contributions to presidential, congressional, and state and local committees and candidates. More than 1,300 contributors are included. Contributors are arranged alphabetically. Also given are the home and business addresses, profession, and business affiliation. CRF has gathered data on individuals who made contributions of more than $10,000 in presidential election years since 1960. This data has been published in Herbert E. Alexander's quadrennial series, *Financing the ... Election.* Four volumes in all have been published, covering the 1960, 1964, 1968, and 1972 elections.

Citizens' Research Foundation. *Studies in Political Finance.* No. 1, 1960–.

Twenty-four studies in this series have been published. These studies tend to be very specific, usually examining a single state or election. As research studies, these offer examples of directions that analysis of political contributions can take. The first twenty-one studies have also been published in a three-volume series by CRF, *Studies in Money in Politics,* edited by Herbert E. Alexander.

U.S. Congress. House. *The Annual Statistical Report of Contributions and Expenditures Made during the 1972 Election Campaigns for the U.S. House of Representatives,* compiled by W. Pat Jennings, as Clerk of the House of Representatives and Supervisory Officier. Doc. No. 93–284. Washington, D.C.: G.P.O., 1974.

This annual contains three main sections and two appendixes: (1) receipts and expenditures for candidates and political committees supporting a single candidate, arranged alphabetically by state and by district number; (2) receipts and expenditures for political committees supporting two or more candidates, arranged alphabetically by committee; (3) individual contributions in excess of $100, arranged alphabetically by surname of contributor or committee, including the address of the contributor and date of the contribution. Appendix A is an alphabetical list of candidates and their supporting political committees. Appendix B is an alphabetical list of political committees and the candidates they supported.

U.S. Congress. Senate. *The Annual Statistical Report of Receipts and Expenditures Made in Connection with Elections for the U.S. Senate in 1972.* Washington, D.C.: G.P.O., 1975.

This report is divided into five sections. The first section includes amounts reported by all Senate candidates and associated committees which support one candidate. This section is arranged by state. Within state breakdowns, committees are listed according to party and candidate. The next section records amounts reported by all political committees supporting more than one candidate. This section is arranged alphabetically by committee. The list of candidates supported is found in Appendix B. The third section, arranged alphabetically by contributor, presents itemized receipts over $100 received by committees and candidates as reported to the Secretary of the Senate for 1972. Receipts are coded according to (1) individual contributions, (2) sales and collections, (3) loans received, (4) other receipts, and (5) transfers. Appendix A is the committee to candidate cross-index. Appendix B is the candidate to committee cross-index. The last two sections provide cross-indexing of sections I, II, and III. Provided also is a cross-index by state and party. The House and Senate volumes use the same format, which makes it easy to use the two together for comparative purposes.

Common Cause. Campaign Finance Monitoring Project. *1972 Federal Campaign Finances.* 10 vols. Washington, D.C.: Common Cause, 1974.

A summary of the campaign finances of every major candidate for Congress in the 1972 general election. The study is organized into ten volumes, divided by region: (1) *New England States,* (2) *Mid-Atlantic States,* (3) *Border States,* (4) *Southeastern States,* (5) *Southern States,* (6) *Southwestern States,* (7) *West Coast States,* (8) *Mountain States,* (9) *Plains States,* and (10) *Great Lake States.* Each volume contains data on three areas of a candidate's campaign finances: (1) a summary of campaign financial data, (2) listing of registered special interest and national political party committees and their contributions, and (3) a list of large contributions from individuals. A five-volume set, the *1974 Congressional Campaign Finances,* has also been published by Common Cause.

Common Cause. Campaign Finance Monitoring Project. *1972 Federal Campaign Finances: Interest Groups and Political Parties.* 3 vols. Washington, D.C.: Common Cause, 1974.

This work provides the finances of all nationally registered political committees which contributed $5,000 or more to federal candidates in 1972. The lists of political committees have been arranged into three volumes: (1) *Business, Agriculture and Dairy, Health;* (2) *Labor;* and (3) *Miscellaneous, Democratic, Republican.* Each of the volumes contains (1) a detailed table of contents, covering the interest groups for that volume, (2) a financial summary for each interest committee, including a brief description of the group or interest that the committee represents and its activities in the 1972 elections, (3) a complete listing of every individual and group which received contributions from the committee and the amount received, and (4) an index listing the name and affiliation of all political committees registered during 1972.

The Federal Election Commission, using information based on financial disclosure provisions of the 1977 House and Senate ethics codes, has initiated a new series, the *FEC Disclosure Series.* Congressional Quarterly also publishes various studies based on Common Cause and federal data.

Campaign Communication

In the age of electronic media, image-makers are becoming perhaps more important than the candidates themselves. Sophisticated public relations firms package and sell candidates. Without doubt there is a very obvious connection between a candidate's financial assets and his ability to get maximum radio and television exposure. There is not an abundance of statistical information on communications, but there are some important sources of data.

Federal Communications Commission. *Survey of Political Broadcasting.* Washington, D.C., 1960–.

This series contains data on primaries and general elections obtained through questionnaires sent to broadcast stations, including AM and FM radio stations and television stations. The information covers several major areas of interest: (1) overall political broadcast activity, (2) charges for political broadcasts, (3) political broadcast activity with respect to specified offices, and (4) editorializing. The 1970 editions of the *Survey of Political Broadcasting* is contained in the following hearings: U.S. Senate, Committee on Commerce, *The Federal Election Campaign Act of 1971.* Hearings before a subcommittee on communication of the Committee on Commerce, Senate, on S.1, S.382, and S.956, 92d Cong., 1st Sess., 1971.

Rosenbloom, David, ed. *The Political Marketplace.* New York: Quadrangle Books, 1972.

This directory is intended as a guide to campaign information for political candidates, but it also serves as an excellent reference work. Although it was written solely for the 1972 elections, it continues to be a valuable source of information. The book is a large compendium of campaign services and a directory to (1) campaign management and counseling firms, (2) political advertising and public relations firms, (3) computer-list and direct mail houses, (4) television and radio time buyers, (5) media outlets and film producers, (6) telephone consultants, (7) demographic and audience research firms, and (8) numerous other aspects of campaign management.

Kaid, Lynda Lee; Keith R. Sanders; and Robert O. Hirsch. *Political Campaign Communication: A Bibliography and Guide to the Literature.* Metuchen, N.J.: Scarecrow, 1974.

A general bibliography on the communication process in political campaigns. The bibliography contains over 1,500 entries, the majority of which are unannotated. It covers 1950 to 1972 and includes books, articles, government documents, pamphlets, and dissertations. The bibliography is indexed. The citations cover analytical and evaluative articles, public opinion polling, media use and expenditures, and all aspects of the communication process.

Public Opinion

The public opinion survey is a rather recent development in social science research. There are several ways to find a wealth of information dealing with polls focusing on congressional campaigns and elections.

Gallup, George Horace. *The Gallup Poll: Public Opinion, 1935–1971.* 3 vols. New York: Random House, 1972.

A complete collection of the Gallup polls from 1935 to 1971. An index in the third volume provides easy subject access. Included in Volume I are three essays by Paul Terry on election survey methods in general and the Gallup poll election survey techniques in particular: "Election Survey Procedures of the Gallup Poll," pp. xi–xxii; "Gallup Poll Election Survey Experience, 1950–1960," pp. xxiii–xxx; "Election Survey Methods," pp. xxxi–xliv.

Gallup, George Horace. *The Gallup Poll: Public Opinion, 1972–1977.* Wilmington, Del.: Scholarly Resources, 1978.

Gallup Opinion Index Report: Political, Social and Economic Trends. Rept. no. 1, June 1965–.

Publishes data generated by the American Institute of Public Opinion and Gallup affiliates. The report is published monthly, with special issues from time to time.

Public Opinion. Washington, D.C.: American Enterprise Institute for Public Policy Research, 1978–.

Provides the results of recent surveys conducted by numerous opinion organizations, including the Canadian Institute of Public Opinion, Harris survey, and the Gallup poll.

National Opinion Research Center. *Bibliography of Publicatons, 1941–1960: Supplement, 1961–December 1971.* Chicago: National Opinion Research Center, 1972.
A complete listing of publications contained within the NORC Library, including many studies on primaries and elections, arranged by both author and subject.

The Harris Survey Yearbook of Public Opinion. New York: Louis Harris and Associates, 1970–.
Each annual volume contains the Harris polls for that year. Since Harris polls are conducted for the *Washington Post* syndicate and *Newsweek,* it is also possible to track down Harris polls through indexes. The *Washington Post* is indexed in *Newspaper Index, Newsweek* in *Reader's Guide.* The results of surveys conducted for publication, as well as reprints, are available from Louis Harris and Associates.

Guides to Statistics

Other important sources of election statistics are provided by numerous state agencies. Within each state there are various departments and organizations that collect data relating to many different aspects of campaigning and electioneering.
The guides listed below identify where to find state election results, demographic data, and socioeconomic information.
Press, Charles, and Oliver Williams. *State Manuals, Blue Books and Election Results.* Berkeley: Institute of Governmental Studies, University of California, 1962.

87

Burnham, Walter Dean. *Sources of Historical Election Data: A Preliminary Bibliography.* East Lansing: Institute for Community Development and Services, Michigan State University, 1963.

U.S. Department of Commerce, Bureau of the Census. *Directory of Non-Federal Statistics for State and Local Areas: A Guide of Sources, 1969.* Washington, D.C., 1970.

U.S. Department of Commerce, Bureau of the Census. *Directory of Federal Statistics for Local Areas: A Guide to Sources, 1976.* Washington, D.C., 1978.

Council of State Governments. *State Blue Books and Reference Publications: A Selected Bibliography.* Rev. and annotated ed. Lexington, Ky.: Council of State Governments, 1974.

Research Centers

There are a number of research centers, foundations, and private institutions which study congressional activities. The following represent the major institutions whose work includes the Congress. Addresses are also given for the agencies or organizations whose publications have been referred to in the preceding sections.

American Enterprise Institute for Public Policy
 Research
1150 17th St., N.W.
Washington, D.C.   20036
Tel: (202) 296-5616

American Institute for Political Communication
402 Prudential Bdg.
Washington, D.C.   20005
Tel: (202) 783-6373

American Institute of Public Opinion
53 Bank St.
Princeton, N.J.   08541
Tel: (609) 924-9600

Americans for Democratic Action
1424 16th St., N.W.
Washington, D.C.   20036
Tel: (202) 265-5771

Bill Status Office
2401A Rayburn House Office Bdg.
Washington, D.C.   20515
Tel: (202) 225-1772

The Brookings Institution
1775 Massachusetts Ave., N.W.
Washington, D.C.   20036
Tel: (202) 483-8919

Center for Public Financing of Elections
201 Massachusetts Ave., N.W.
Washington, D.C.   20002
Tel: (202) 546-5511

Citizens' Research Foundation
245 Nassau St.
Princeton, N.J.   08540
Tel: (609) 924-0246

Clerk of the House of Representatives
H–105 Capitol Bdg.
Washington, D.C.   20515
Tel: (202) 225-7000

Commerce Department
Bureau of the Census
Population Division
Washington, D.C.   20233
Tel: (202) 763-5161

Common Cause
2030 M St., N.W.
Washington, D.C.   20036
Tel: (202) 833-1200

Congressional Budget Office
Second and D Sts., S.W.
Washington, D.C.   20515
Tel: (202) 225-4416

Congressional Information Service
7101 Wisconsin Ave.
Washington, D.C.   20014
Tel: (301) 654-1550

Congressional Quarterly, Inc.
1414 22nd St., N.W.
Washington, D.C.   20037
Tel: (202) 296-6800

Congressional Record Office
H–112 Capitol Bdg.
Washington, D.C.   20515
Tel: (202) 225-2100

Democratic National Committee
1625 Massachusetts Ave., N.W.
Washington, D.C.   20036
Tel: (202) 797-5900

Elections Research Center
1619 Massachusetts Ave., N.W.
Washington, D.C.   20036
Tel: (202) 387-6066

Fair Campaign Practices Committee
613 Pennsylvania Ave., S.E.
Washington, D.C.   20003
Tel: (202) 544-5656

Federal Communications Commission
1919 M St., N.W.
Washington, D.C.   20554
Tel: (202) 655-4000

Federal Election Commission
1325 K St., N.W.
Washington, D.C.   20463
Tel: (202) 382-5162

Friends Committee on National Legislation
245 2nd St., N.E.
Washington, D.C.   20002
Tel: (202) 547-4343

General Accounting Office
441 G St., N.W.
Washington, D.C.   20548
Tel: (202) 386-4949

Government Printing Office
Congressional Desk
North Capitol and H Sts., N.W.
Washington, D.C.   20401
Tel: (202) 376-2030

Governmental Affairs Institute
1776 Massachusetts Ave., N.W.
Washington, D.C.   20036
Tel: (202) 833-2500

Institute of Election Administration
American University
Washington, D.C.   20016
Tel: (202) 676-2350

Inter-University Consortium for Political and Social Research
P.O. Box 1248
Ann Arbor, Mich.   48106
Tel: (313) 764-2570

Joint Center for Political Studies
1426 H St., N.W.
Washington, D.C.   20005
Tel: (202) 638-4477

Laboratory for Political Research
Regional Social Science Data Archive
University of Iowa
321A Schaeffer Hall
Iowa City, Iowa   52240
Tel: (319) 353-3945

Library of Congress
Congressional Research Service
10 1st St., S.E.
Washington, D.C.   20554
Tel: (202) 426-5770

Louis Harris and Associates
1270 Avenue of the Americas
New York, N.Y.   10020
Tel: (212) 245-7414

National Committee for an Effective Congress
201 Massachusetts Ave., N.E.
Washington, D.C.   20002
Tel: (202) 833-4000

National Opinion Research Center
University of Chicago
6036 South Ellis Ave.
Chicago, Ill. 60637
Tel: (312) 752-6444

Public Citizen, Inc.
1346 Connecticut Ave.
Washington, D.C.   20036
Tel: (202) 293-9142

Republican National Committee
310 1st St., S.E.
Washington, D.C.   20003
Tel: (202) 484-6500

Roper Public Opinion Research Center
Williams College
Williamstown, Mass.   01267
Tel: (413) 458-7131, ext. 271

Secretary of the Senate
S-221 Capitol Bdg.
Washington, D.C.   20501
Tel: (202) 224-2115

Senate Historical Office
United States Senate
Washington, D.C.   20510
Tel: (202) 224-6900

For information concerning current activities of these organizations, write directly to the organization, most of which are listed in one of the following directories:

Congressional Quarterly. *Washington Information Directory*. Washington, D.C.: Congressional Quarterly, 1975–.

A thoroughly indexed guide to over 5,000 information sources in Congress, the executive branch, and nongovernmental organizations. This annual directory helps the researcher make some sense out of the maze of agencies, institutes, associations, and foundations in the Washington area. In addition to the standard organizational information, a concise statement spells out the committee's, organization's, or agency's activities. A chapter on Congress lists, in addition to congressional offices and organizations, numerous citizens' interest groups like Ralph Nader's Public Citizen, Inc., Americans for Democratic Action, and the National Committee for an Effective Congress. These organizations seek to bring about

93

change in congressional procedures, monitor legislative proposals, and rate individual voting performances on issues such as tax reform, budget control, military spending, consumer protection. Many public interest groups distribute newsletters and other materials free of charge or for a nominal fee. It is certainly worthwhile to write to organizations asking about their activities and what publications are available to the public. The *Directory* is indexed by subject and agency.

United States. Congress. House. Commission on Information and Facilities. *Inventory of Information Resources and Services Available to the U.S. House of Representatives, Parts I–IV.* Westport, Conn.: Greenwood Press, 1977. [Reprint of 1976 edition.]

An excellent guide to internal sources of congressional information on the legislative process, managing congressional offices, and the organization and operation of Congress. Also describes the resources of the Congressional Budget Office, General Accounting Office, Government Printing Office, Library of Congress, and Office of Technology Assessment. The last two parts of the compendium discuss executive branch information resources and private organization information services.

Library Collections

Large academic libraries and research institutions will probably have most of the reference works discussed in this guide. Smaller libraries usually cannot afford to purchase all the guides to congressional research.

Most libraries will have *CIS/INDEX* and its *ANNUAL,* but not all libraries will subscribe to the *Congressional Monitor* or *Congressional Index.* Large university libraries will usually have all the journals, statistical sources, directories, and other works cited earlier.

The size of a library's document collection can range from limited vertical files to vast mountainous holdings. The Depository Library Act of 1962 represented a major effort in establishing a national system of federal document collections. There are two kinds of depositories, regional and selective. Regional depositories receive copies of all documents authorized for distribution under the program, while selective depositories receive only what they decide to collect. Thousands of libraries not part of the depository system have document collections, but their holdings may not be sufficient in all instances. To locate the name of the nearest depository library and the date it was designated as such, consult the most recent September issue of the *Monthly Catalog of United States Government Publications*. The depository libraries are listed alphabetically by state and by city within each state. The depository system also makes it possible to acquire documents through interlibrary loan. In addition to the depository libraries, there are numerous library collections housed in various federal agencies in Washington and around the country. Mildred Benton's *Federal Library Resources: A User's Guide to Research Collections* (New York: Science Associates International, 1973) provides valuable information about many federal libraries. The Government Documents Round Table of the American Library Association has compiled *Directory of Government Document Collections and Librarians,* 2d ed. (Washington, D.C.: Congressional Information Service, 1978), which is especially useful for obtaining the names and addresses of librarians who administer federal document collections.

Large libraries often have segregated document collections, whereas smaller institutions tend to incorporate documents into the library's holdings. In the latter case, government publications are classified in the same fashion as the entire collection. Consequently, documents are distributed throughout the library. Since separate document collections can be administered in various ways, it is not uncommon for libraries to catalog and classify government publications according to their own distinctive schemes.

Libraries are not merely warehouses where materials are stored. A library consists of specialists trained to assist patrons in learning how to use the library and retrieve information. A library patron should not hesitate to ask a librarian for help, whether for an explanation of a reference tool, classification system, or how to locate an item on the shelf. It is the responsibility of librarians to aid patrons. Students or researchers should not feel they are bothering a librarian.

Legislative Research Guides

There are many excellent guides for the researcher who wants a more exhaustive analysis of the legislative process and the research tools by which to trace legislation. These sources are invaluable for techniques concerning retrospective tracing. This is especially true for legislation preceding 1940. Tracing legislation enacted during the eighteenth and nineteenth centuries requires consulting a number of special tools. The guides listed below will direct the researcher to the proper tools needed for researching legislation in earlier time periods. Once the researcher has learned the rudiments of legal research and become acquainted with the legislative process by actually tracing bills through Congress, he may wish to consult these works to better understand the more specialized research tools and congressional publications.

Bitner, Harry, and Miles O. Price. *Effective Legal Research*. 3d ed. Boston: Little, Brown, 1969.

An excellent description of the legislative process and all tools related to legal research. Provides an in-depth examination and explanation of the reference works and indexes used in legislative tracing.

Folsom, Gwendolyn B. *Legislative History: Research for the Interpretation of Laws*. Charlottesville: University Press of Virginia, 1972.

A well-written handbook for beginning researchers. The work contains important chapters on the history of the legislative process, basic sources of information documenting the process, and a step-by-step method of researching legislative histories.

Morehead, Joe. *Introduction to United States Public Documents.* Littleton, Colo.: Libraries Unlimited, 1975.
This work is a textbook for library school students and professional librarians; it is also a valuable guide for anyone interested in researching federal documents. The chapter on legislative branch materials contains a wealth of information. This chapter gives an especially detailed description of congressional publications and the reference tools used in tracing legislation.

Boyd, Anne Morris. *United States Government Publications.* 3d ed. Revised by Rae Elizabeth Rips. New York: Wilson, 1949.
Even though this work is somewhat out-dated, its discussion of congressional publications is still useful for understanding the nature, types, and value of congressional publications. The work is also important when researching congressional publications of the eighteenth and nineteenth centuries.

Schmeckebeir, Laurence F., and Roy B. Eastin. *Government Publications and Their Use.* 2d rev. ed. Washington, D.C.: Brookings Institution, 1969.
A well-known and respected reference work covering all government publications. Contains extensive information on all forms of publications published under the authority of Congress. Although the work includes much information not found elsewhere, it does not provide a straightforward strategy for legislative tracing.

Meyer, Evelyn S. "Reference Guides to Congressional Research," *RQ* 22, no. 1 (Fall 1972): 30–36.
A short guide to sources of information on the Congress and tools used for legislative tracing. Each source is briefly annotated, providing a synoptic description of its value and general format.

Shannon, Michael Owen. *To Trace a Law: Use of Library Materials in a Classroom Exercise.* ERIC Document ED 111 341. Bronx, N.Y.: Herbert H. Lehman College Library, City University of New York, 1975.

A basic guide to legislative history for the novice. The guide is designed to familiarize students with the legislative process by asking them to choose a topic of interest and trace a bill as it becomes law. The guide provides descriptions of the standard reference works with which the student can find information on laws, legislators, and legislative procedures.

Nabors, Eugene. "Legislative History and Government Documents—Another Step in Legal Research," *Government Publications Review* 3, no. 1 (Spring 1976): 15–41.
The author presents a formula approach to developing legislative histories. All of the actions involved in the legislative process are perceived as the behavior of a system. The author has constructed an abstract model representing the legislative process, which can be used as a means to charting legislative histories.
There are many other research guides to political science and government publications which also contain sections or chapters on congressional research. Look for most of these guides in any college or university library.
American Library Association. Government Documents Roundtable. Education Task Force. *Draft Syllabus of Resources for Teaching Government Publications*. Chicago: Government Documents Roundtable, 1976.

Brock, Clifton. *The Literature of Political Science: A Guide for Students, Librarians and Teachers*. New York: R. R. Bowker, 1969. [Chapter 5, "United States Government Publications," pp. 33–49.]

Holler, Frederick L. *The Information Sources of Political Science*. 5 vols. Santa Barbara: ABC-Clio, 1975. [Volume 3, *American Government and Politics, United States Public Law and International Law.*]

Freides, Thelma. "A Guide to Information Sources on Federal Government Agencies," *News for Teachers of Political Science* 18 (Summer 1978): 6–13.

Mason, John Brown. *Research Resources: Annotated Guide to the Social Sciences*. 2 vols. Santa Barbara: ABC-Clio, 1968–1971. [Volume 2, *Official Publications:*

U.S. Government, United Nations, International Organizations and Statistical Sources.]

Lu, Joseph K. *U.S. Government Publications Relating to the Social Sciences: A Selected Annotated Guide.* Beverly Hills: Sage, 1975. [Chapter V, "Congress," pp. 77–88.]

Palic, Vladimir M. *Government Publications: A Guide to Bibliographic Tools.* 4th ed. Washington, D.C.: G.P.O., 1975. ["Federal Government," pp. 11–80.]

Vose, Clement E. *A Guide to Library Resources in Political Science: American Government.* Instructional Resource Monograph no. 1. Washington, D.C.: American Political Science Association, 1975. ["Congress," pp. 33–42.]

Weinhaus, Carol, ed. *Bibliographic Tools: Volume II, Legislative Guide.* Working paper. Cambridge: Program on Information Technologies and Public Policy, Harvard University, 1976.

Tracing legislation is much easier today. Commerical publishers have started to provide greater bibliographic control of government publications than was formerly true of government produced indexes. Congressional Information Service's *CIS/INDEX*, Carrollton Press's *Cumulative Subject Index to the Monthly Catalog of U.S. Government Publications,* and other new reference tools have made it easier to trace legislation. Nonetheless, legislative research requires time and patience.

In this guide I have touched upon almost every aspect of legislative tracing and research. I have not discussed every available reference work, and have only briefly mentioned others. It is not unusual for a student to spend hours researching, only later to find out by accident that if he had used a particular bibliographic tool, he could have saved considerable time. Almost every researcher has had the experience of serendipitously discovering a new reference tool. The main reason for compiling this guide was to systematically present the basic tools used in legislative tracing in a clear and concise manner. I hope this guide has made researchers more aware of the resources available.

Appendix A: Citing Government Publications

When students use government documents in their research, they are often unsure of how to cite them. Below I have cited the publications relating to the Privacy Act of 1974 as they would appear in a bibliography. Footnotes would also provide the specific page cited. There are various formats for citing government publications in bibliographies and footnotes, but regardless of stylistic variations, all citations should include the basic information. For congressional publications, it is necessary to record the chamber, committee, title, type of document (i.e., report, committee print, etc.), Congress and session, and date. When citing executive branch publications, include the department, agency or office, title, personal author if applicable, publisher, and date.

BILLS

U.S. Congress. House. H.R. 16373, *A Bill to Safeguard Individual Privacy from the Misuse of Federal Records and....* 93d Cong., 2d Sess., 1974.

U.S. Congress. Senate. S. 3418, *A Bill to Establish a Federal Privacy Board....* 93d Cong., 2d Sess., 1974.

U.S. Congress. Senate. Committee on Government Operations. Ad Hoc Subcommittee on Privacy and Information Systems. Committee on the Judiciary. Subcommittee on Constitutional Rights. *Privacy: The Collection, Use and Computerization of Personal Data.* Joint Hearing on S. 3418.... 93d Cong., 2d Sess. Washington, D.C.: G.P.O., 1974.

U. S. Congress. Senate. Committee on Government Operations. *Materials Pertaining to S. 3418 and Protecting Individual Privacy in Federal Gathering, Use, and Disclosure of Information.* Committee print. 93d Cong., 2d Sess., Washington, D.C.: G.P.O., 1974.

U.S. Congress. House. Committee on Government Operations. *Privacy Act of 1974.* H. Rept. 93–1416. 93d Cong., 2d Sess., 1974.

U.S. Congress. Senate. Committee on Government Operations. *Preservation, Protection, and Public Access with Respect to Certain Tape Recordings and Other Materials.* S. Rept. 93–1416. 93d Cong., 2d Sess., 1974.

Note that citations to the vote differ.
Congressional Record, 93d Cong., 2d Sess., Nov. 21, 1974, 120, S19858. [Daily edition.]

Congressional Record, 93d Cong., 2d Sess., 1974, 120, 36917. [Bound volume.]

Journal of the Senate, 93d Cong., 2d Sess., 1974, 1475. [Bound volume.]

Appendix A: Citing Government Publications

PRESIDENTIAL STATEMENT OF OCTOBER 9, 1974

Note that citations to the same statement in the *Weekly Compilation of Presidential Documents* and *Public Papers of the President* differ.

U.S. President. "Right of Privacy Legislation [Oct. 9, 1974]," *Weekly Compilation of Presidential Documents* 10, no. 41 (Oct. 14, 1974): 1250.

U.S. President. "Statement on Privacy Legislation [Oct. 9, 1974]," *Public Papers of the Presidents of the United States: Gerald R. Ford (1974)*. U.S. National Archives and Records Administration. Washington, D.C.: G.P.O., 1975, pp. 243–44.

LAW

Pub. L. 93–579 (Dec. 31, 1974), *Privacy Act of 1974*. 88 Stat. 1896.

EXECUTIVE PUBLICATIONS

U.S. Department of Health, Education and Welfare. Secretary's Advisory Committee on Automated Personal Data Systems. *Records, Computers and the Rights of Citizens*. DHEW Pub. No. (05)73–94. Washington, D.C.: G.P.O., 1973.

U.S. President's Domestic Council. Committee on the Right of Privacy. *Privacy, A Public Concern: A Resource Document*. Edited by Kent S. Larsen. Washington, D.C.: G.P.O., 1975.

While there are abbreviated formats for citing government publications, it is always best to provide as complete a bibliographic entry as possible. When footnoting, using abbreviations can save considerable space and be an effective shorthand; but it is important to be consistent in one's use of abbreviations. The best guides to the use of abbreviations are *Effective Legal Research* (see p. 95) and *A Uniform System of Citation,* sold by the Harvard Law Review Association, Gannett House, Cambridge, Mass. 02138.

For additional information on citing government publications, consult Kate L. Turabian's *A Manual for Writers of Term Papers, Theses, and Dissertations,* University of Chicago, *A Manual of Style,* 12th ed., or George D. Brightbill and Wayne C. Maxson's *Citation Manual for United States Publications,* Study Guide and Teaching Aids, Paper no. 10 (Philadelphia: Center for Study of Federalism, Temple University, 1974). No matter what style you use in citing government publications, be consistent. Supply the same information in the same order and format.

Appendix B: Despository Libraries for United States Public Documents

Designated Regional Libraries receive one copy of all U.S. publications made available to depository libraries. All other libraries select classes of publications they wish to receive. The date following the name of the library is the year the library became a depository.

ALABAMA

Alexander City	Alexander City State Junior College, Thomas D. Russell Library (1967)
Auburn	Auburn University, Ralph Brown Draughon Library (1907)
Birmingham	Birmingham Public Library (1895)
	Birmingham-Southern College Library (1932)
	Jefferson State Junior College, James B. Allen Library (1970)
	Samford University, Harwell G. Davis Library (1884)

Enterprise	Enterprise State Junior College Library (1967)
Florence	University of North Alabama, Collier Library (1932)
Gadsden	Gadsden Public Library (1963)
Huntsville	University of Alabama in Huntsville, Huntsville Campus Library (1964)
Jacksonville	Jacksonville State University, Romana Wood Library (1929)
Maxwell A.F. Base	Air University Library (1963)
Mobile	Mobile Public Library (1963)
	Spring Hill College, Thomas Byrne Memorial Library (1937)
	University of South Alabama Library (1968)
Montgomery	Alabama State Department of Archives and History Library (1884)
	Alabama Supreme Court and State Law Library (1884)
	Auburn University at Montgomery Library (1971)—regional
Normal	Alabama Agricultural and Mechanical University, Drake Memorial Library (1963)
St. Bernard	St. Bernard College Library (1962)
Troy	Troy State University, Lurleen B. Wallace Educational Resources Center (1963)
Tuskegee Institute	Tuskegee Institute, Hollis Burke Frissell Library (1907)
University	University of Alabama, Library (1860)—regional
	University of Alabama, School of Law Library (1967)

ALASKA

Anchorage	University of Alaska, Anchorage Library (1961)
	Supreme Court of Alaska Library (1973)
College	University of Alaska, Elmer E. Rasmuson Library (1922)

Juneau	Alaska State Library (1964)
Ketchikan	Ketchikan Community College Library (1970)

ARIZONA

Coolidge	Central Arizona College, Instructional Materials Center (1973)
Flagstaff	Northern Arizona University Library (1937)
Phoenix	Department of Library and Archives—regional
	Phoenix Public Library (1917)
Prescott	Yavapai College Library (1976)
Tempe	Arizona State University, Matthews Library (1944)
Thatcher	Eastern Arizona College Library (1976)
Tucson	Tucson Public Library (1970)
	University of Arizona Library (1907)—regional
Yuma	Yuma City-County Library (1963)

ARKANSAS

Arkadelphia	Ouachita Baptist University, Riley Library (1963)
Batesville	Arkansas College Library (1963)
Clarksville	College of the Ozarks Library (1925)
Conway	Hendrix College, O. C. Bailey Library (1903)
Fayetteville	University of Arkansas Library (1907)
Little Rock	Arkansas Supreme Court Library (1962)
	Little Rock Public Library (1953)
	University of Arkansas at Little Rock, Library (1973)
Magnolia	Southern Arkansas University, Mogale Library (1956)
Monticello	University of Arkansas at Monticello Library (1956)
Pine Bluff	University of Arkansas, Watson Memorial Library (1976)
Russellville	Arkansas Tech University, Tomlinson Library (1925)

Searcy	Harding College, Beaumont Memorial Library (1963)
State University	Arkansas State University, Dean B. Ellis Library (1913)
Walnut Ridge	Southern Baptist College, Felix Goodson Library (1967)

CALIFORNIA

Anaheim	Anaheim Public Library (1963)
Arcadia	Arcadia Public Library (1975)
Arcata	Humboldt State College Library (1963)
Bakersfield	California State College at Bakersfield, Bakersfield Library (1974)
	Kern County Library (1943)
Berkeley	University of California, Berkeley, General Library (1907)
	University of California, Berkeley, Law Library, Earl Warren Legal Center (1963)
Carson	Carson Regional Library (1973)
Chico	Chico State University Library (1962)
Claremont	Pomona College Documents Collection, Honnold Library (1913)
Compton	Compton Library (1972)
Culver City	Culver City Library (1966)
Davis	University of California, Davis, Library (1953)
	University of California, Davis, School of Law Library (1972)
Dominguez Hills	California State College, Dominguez Hills, Educational Resources Center (1973)
Downey	Downey City Library (1963)
Fresno	California State University Library (1962)
	Fresno County Free Library (1920)
Fullerton	California State University at Fullerton Library (1963)
Garden Grove	Garden Grove Regional Library (1963)
Gardena	Gardena Public Library (1966)
Hayward	California State College at Hayward Library (1963)

Huntington Park	Huntington Park Library, San Antonio Region (1970)
Inglewood	Inglewood Public Library (1963)
Irvine	University of California, Irvine, Library (1963)
La Jolla	University of California, San Diego, University Library (1963)
Lakewood	Angelo Iacoboni Public Library (1970)
Lancaster	Lancaster Regional Library (1967)
Long Beach	California State College at Long Beach Library (1962)
	Long Beach Public Library (1933)
Los Angeles	California State College at Los Angeles, John F. Kennedy Memorial Library (1956)
	Los Angeles County Law Library (1963)
	Los Angeles Public Library (1891)
	Loyola University of Los Angeles Library (1933)
	Occidental College, Mary Norton Clapp Library (1941)
	Pepperdine University Library (1963)
	Southwestern University, School of Law Library (1975)
	University of California, Los Angeles, Law Library (1958)
	University of California, Los Angeles, Library (1932)
	University of Southern California Library (1933)
Menlo Park	Department of the Interior, Geological Survey Library (1962)
Montebello	Montebello Library (1966)
Monterey	Naval Postgraduate School Library (1963)
Monterey Park	Bruggemeyer Memorial Library (1964)
Northridge	California State University at Northridge Library (1958)
Norwalk	Los Cerritos Regional Library (1973)
Oakland	Mills College Library (1966)
	Oakland Public Library (1923)

109

Ontario	Ontario City Library (1974)
Pasadena	California Institute of Technology, Milikan Memorial Library (1933)
Pleasant Hill	Contra Costa County Library (1964)
Redding	Shasta County Library (1956)
Redlands	University of Redlands, Armacost Library (1933)
Redwood City	Redwood City Public Library (1966)
Reseda	West Valley Regional Branch Library (1966)
Richmond	Richmond Public Library (1943)
Riverside	Riverside Public Library (1947)
	University of California, Riverside, Library (1963)
Sacramento	California State Library (1895)—regional
	Sacramento City-County Library (1880)
	Sacramento County Law Library (1963)
	Sacramento State College Library (1963)
San Bernardino	San Bernardino County Free Library (1964)
San Diego	San Diego County Law Library (1973)
	San Diego County Library (1895)
	San Diego Public Library (1895)
	San Diego State University, Love Library (1962)
	University of San Diego Law Library (1967)
San Francisco	Mechanics' Institute Library (1889)
	San Francisco Public Library (1889)
	San Francisco State College, Social Science and Business Library (1955)
	Supreme Court of California Library (1972)
	U. S. Court of Appeals for Ninth Circuit Library (1971)
	University of San Francisco, Richard A. Gleeson Library (1963)
San Jose	San Jose State College Library (1962)
San Leandro	San Leandro Community Library Center (1961)

San Luis Obispo	California State Polytechnic University Library (1969)
San Rafael	Marin County Free Library (1975)
Santa Ana	Orange County Law Library (1975)
	Santa Ana Public Library (1959)
Santa Barbara	University of California, Santa Barbara, Library (1960)
Santa Rosa	Santa Rosa-Sonoma County Public Library (1896)
Stanford	Stanford University Libraries (1895)
Stockton	Public Library of Stockton and San Joaquin County (1884)
Thousand Oaks	California Lutheran College Library (1964)
Torrance	Torrance Civic Center Library (1969)
Turlock	Stanislaus State College Library (1964)
Valencia	Valencia Regional Library (1972)
Van Nuys	Los Angeles Valley College Library (1970)
Ventura	Ventura County Library Services Agency (1975)
Visalia	Tulare County Free Library (1967)
Walnut	Mount San Antonio College Library (1966)
West Covina	West Covina Library (1966)
Whittier	Whittier College, Wardman Library (1963)

CANAL ZONE

Balboa Heights	Canal Zone Library-Museum (1963)

COLORADO

Alamosa	Adams State College Learning Resources Center (1963)
Boulder	University of Colorado Libraries (1879)—regional
Colorado Springs	Colorado College, Charles Leaming Tutt Library (1880)
	University of Colorado, Colorado Springs Library (1974)

Denver	Colorado State Library (unknown)
	Denver Pubic Library (1884)—regional
	Department of the Interior, Bureau of Reclamation Library (1962)
	Regis College, Dayton Memorial Library (1915)
	U. S. Court of Appeals, Tenth Circuit Library (1973)
	University of Denver, Penrose Library (1909)
Fort Collins	Colorado State University Library (1907)
Golden	Colorado School of Mines, Arthur Lakes Library (1939)
Grand Junction	Mesa County Public Library (1975)
Greeley	University of Northern Colorado Library (1966)
Gunnison	Western State College, Leslie J. Savage Library (1932)
La Junta	Otero Junior College, Wheeler Library (1963)
Lakewood	Jefferson County Public Library, Lakewood Regional Library (1968)
Pueblo	Pueblo Regional Library (1893)
	University of Southern Colorado Library (1965)
U. S. Air Force Academy	Academy Library (1956)

CONNECTICUT

Bridgeport	Bridgeport Public Library (1884)
Danbury	Western Connecticut State College, Ruth A. Haas Library (1967)
Danielson	Quinebaug Valley Community College (1975)
Enfield	Enfield Public Library (1967)
Hartford	Connecticut State Library (unknown)—regional
	Hartford Public Library (1945)
	Trinity College Library (1895)
Middletown	Wesleyan University Library (1906)

Mystic	Marine Historical Association, Inc., G. W. Blunt White Library (1964)
New Britain	Central Connecticut State College, Elihu Burritt Library (1973)
New Haven	Southern Connecticut State College Library (1968)
	Yale University Library (1859)
New London	Connecticut College Library (1926)
	U. S. Coast Guard Academy Library (1939)
Stamford	Stamford Public Library (1973)
Storrs	University of Connecticut, Wilbur Cross Library (1907)
Waterbury	Post College, Traurig Library (1977)
	Silas Bronson Library (1869)
West Haven	University of New Haven Library (1971)

DELAWARE

Dover	Delaware State College, William C. Jason Library (1962)
	State Department of Community Affairs and Economic Development, Division of Libraries (1972)
	State Law Library in Kent County (unknown)
Georgetown	Delaware Technical and Community College, Southern Branch Library (1968)
	Sussex County Law Library (1976)
Newark	University of Delaware, Morris Library (1907)
Wilmington	Delaware Law School Library (1976)
	New Castle County Law Library (1974)
	Wilmington Institute and New Castle County Library (1861)

DISTRICT OF COLUMBIA

Washington	Administrative Conference of U. S. Library (1977)

Advisory Commission on
Intergovernmental Relations Library
(1972)

Civil Aeronautics Board Library (1975)

Civil Service Commission Library
(1963)

Department of Commerce Library
(1955)

Department of Health, Education and
Welfare Library (1954)

Department of Housing and Urban
Development Library (1969)

Department of the Interior Central
Library (1895)

Department of Justice Main Library
(1895)

Department of Labor Library (1976)

Department of State Library (1895)

Department of State, Office of Legal
Advisor, Law Library (1966)

Department of Transportation,
National Highway Traffic Safety
Administration (1968)

District of Columbia Public Library
(1943)

Federal City College Library (1970)

Federal Deposit Insurance Corporation
Library (1972)

Federal Election Commission Library
(1975)

Federal Reserve System Law Library
(1976)

General Accounting Office Library
(1975)

General Services Administration
Library (1975)

Georgetown University Library (1969)

Indian Claims Commission Library
(1968)

Library of Congress, Gift and Exchange
Division (1977)

National Defense University Library
(1895)
Navy Department Library (1895)
Navy Department, Office of Judge
Advocate General Library (1963)
Office of Management and Budget
Library (1965)
Office of The Adjutant General,
Department of Army Library (1969)
Postal Service Library (1895)
Treasury Department Library (1895)
U. S. Court of Appeals, Judge's Library
(1975)
Veterans' Administration, Central
Office Library (1976)

FLORIDA

Boca Raton	Florida Atlantic University Library (1963)
Clearwater	Clearwater Public Library (1972)
Coral Gables	University of Miami Library (1939)
Daytona Beach	Volusia County Public Libraries (1963)
De Land	Stetson University, dePont-Ball Library (1887)
Fort Lauderdale	Broward County Library (1976)
	Nova University Law Library (1967)
Fort Pierce	Indian River Community College Library (1975)
Gainesville	University of Florida Libraries (1907)—regional
Jacksonville	Haydon Burns Library (1914)
	Jacksonville University, Swisher Library (1962)
	University of North Florida Library (1972)
Lakeland	Lakeland Public Library (1928)
Leesburg	Lake-Sumter Community College Library (1963)
Melbourne	Florida Institute of Technology Library (1963)

Miami	Florida International University Library (1970)
	Miami Public Library (1952)
North Miami	Florida International University, North Miami Campus Library (1977)
Opa Locka	Biscayne College Library (1966)
Orlando	Florida Technological University Library (1966)
Palatka	St. Johns River Junior College Library (1963)
Pensacola	University of West Florida, John C. Pace Library (1966)
Port Charlotte	Charlotte County Library System (1973)
St. Petersburg	St. Petersburg Public Library (1965)
	Stetson University College Law Library (1975)
Sarasota	Sarasota Public Library (1970)
Tallahassee	Florida Agricultural and Mechanical University, Coleman Memorial Library (1936)
	Florida State University, R. M. Stozier Library (1941)
	Florida Supreme Court Library (1974)
	State Library of Florida (1929)
Tampa	Tampa Public Library (1965)
	University of South Florida Library (1962)
	University of Tampa, Merle Kelce Library (1953)
Winter Park	Rollins College, Mills Memorial Library (1909)

GEORGIA

Albany	Albany Dougherty Public Library (1964)
Americus	Georgia Southwestern College, James Earl Carter Library (1966)
Athens	University of Georgia Libraries (1907)—regional
Atlanta	Atlanta Public Library (1880)

Atlanta University, Trevor Arnett
Library (1962)
Emory University, Robert W. Woodruff
Library (1928)
Emory University, School of Law
Library (1968)
Georgia Institute of Technology, Price
Gilbert Memorial Library (1963)
Georgia State Library (unknown)
Georgia State University Library
(1970)

Augusta — Augusta College Library (1962)
Brunswick — Brunswick Public Library (1965)
Carrollton — West Georgia College, Sanford Library
(1962)
Columbus — Columbus College, Simon Schwob
Memorial Library (1975)
Dahlonega — North Georgia College Library (1939)
Decatur — Dekalb Community College-South
Campus, Learning Resources Center
(1973)
Gainesville — Chestatee Regional Library (1968)
Macon — Mercer University Library (1964)
Marietta — Kennesaw Junior College Library
(1968)
Milledgeville — Georgia College at Milledgeville, Ina
Dillard Russel Library (1950)
Mount Berry — Berry College, Memorial Library (1970)
Savannah — Savannah Public and
Chatham-Effingham Liberty
Regional Library (1857)
Statesboro — Georgia Southern College, Rosenwald
Library (1939)
Valdosta — Valdosta State College, Richard Holmes
Powell Library (1956)

GUAM
Agana — Nieves M. Flores Memorial Library
(1962)

HAWAII

Hilo	University of Hawaii, Hilo Campus Library (1962)
Honolulu	Chaminade College of Honolulu Library (1965)
	Hawaii Medical Library, Inc. (1968)
	Hawaii State Library (1929)
	Municipal Reference Library of the City and County of Honolulu (1965)
	Supreme Court Law Library (1973)
	University of Hawaii Library (1907)—regional
Laie	Church College of Hawaii, Woolley Library (1964)
Lihue	Kauai Public Library (1967)
Pearl City	Leeward Community College Library (1967)
Wailuku	Maui Public Library (1962)

IDAHO

Boise	Boise State College Library (1966)
	Boise Public Library and Information Center (1929)
	Idaho State Law Library (unknown)
	Idaho State Library (1971)
Caldwell	College of Idaho, Terteling Library (1930)
Moscow	University of Idaho Library (1907)—regional
Pocatello	Idaho State University Library (1908)
Rexburg	Ricks College, David O. McKay Library (1946)
Twin Falls	College of Southern Idaho Library (1970)

ILLINOIS

Bloomington	Illinois Wesleyan University Libraries (1964)
Carbondale	Southern Illinois University Library (1932)
Carlinville	Blackburn College Library (1954)

Carterville	Shawnee Library System (1971)
Champaign	University of Illinois Law Library, College of Law (1965)
Charleston	Eastern Illinois University, Booth Library (1962)
Chicago	Chicago Public Library (1876)
	Chicago State University Library (1954)
	De Paul University, Lincoln Park Campus Library (1975)
	Field Museum of Natural History Library (1963)
	John Crerar Library (1909)
	Loyola University, E. M. Cudahy Memorial Library (1966)
	Northeastern Illinois University Library (1961)
	University of Chicago Law Library (1964)
	University of Chicago Library (1897)
	University of Illinois, Chicago Circle Campus Library (1957)
Decatur	Decatur Public Library (1954)
De Kalb	Northern Illinois University, Swen Franklin Parson Library (1960)
Edwardsville	Southern Illinois University, Lovejoy Memorial Library (1959)
Elsah	Principia College, Marshall Brooks Library (1957)
Evanston	Northwestern University Library (1876)
Freeport	Freeport Public Library (1905)
Galesburg	Galesburg Public Library (1896)
Jacksonville	MacMurry College, Henry Pfeiffer Library (1929)
Kankakee	Olivet Nazarene College, Benner Library and Resource Center (1946)
Lake Forest	Lake Forest College, Donnelley Library (1962)
Lebanon	McKendree College, Holman Library (1968)

119

Lisle	Illinois Benedictine College, Theodore F. Lownik Library (1911)
Lockport	Lewis University Library (1952)
Macomb	Western Illinois University Memorial Library (1962)
Moline	Black Hawk College, Learning Resources Center (1970)
Monmouth	Monmouth College Library (1860)
Morton Grove	Oakton Community College Library (1976)
Mt. Carmel	Wabash Valley College Library (1975)
Normal	Illinois State University, Milner Library (187?)
Oak Park	Oak Park Public Library (1963)
Oglesby	Illinos Valley Community College Library (1976)
Palos Hills	Moraine Valley Community College Library (1972)
Park Forest South	Governors State University Library (1974)
Peoria	Bradley University, Cullom Davis Library (1963)
	Peoria Public Library (1883)
River Forest	Rosary College Library (1966)
Rockford	Rockford Public Library (unknown)
Springfield	Illinois State Library (unknown)—regional
Urbana	University of Illinois Library (1907)
Wheaton	Wheaton College Library (1964)
Woodstock	Woodstock Public Library (1963)

INDIANA

Anderson	Anderson College, Charles E. Wilson Library (1959)
Bloomington	Indiana University Library (1881)
Crawfordsville	Wabash College, Lilly Library (1906)
Evansville	Evansville and Vanderburgh County Public Library (1928)
	Indiana State University, Evansville Campus Library (1969)
Fort Wayne	Indiana-Purdue Universities, Regional Campus Library (1965)

	Public Library of Fort Wayne and Allen County (1896)
Franklin	Franklin College Library (1976)
Gary	Gary Public Library (1943)
	Indiana University, Northwest Campus Library (1966)
Greencastle	DePauw University, Roy O. West Library (1879)
Hammond	Hammond Public Library (1964)
Hanover	Hanover College Library (1892)
Huntington	Huntington College Library (1964)
Indianapolis	Butler University, Irwin Library (1965)
	Indiana State Library (unknown)—regional
	Indiana Supreme Court Law Library (1975)
	Indiana University, Law Library (1967)
	Indianapolis-Marion County Public Library (1906)
Kokomo	Indiana University, Kokomo Regional Campus Library (1969)
Lafayette	Purdue University Library (1907)
Muncie	Ball State University Library (1959)
	Muncie Public Library (1906)
New Albany	Indiana University, Southeastern Campus Library (1965)
Notre Dame	University of Notre Dame, Memorial Library (1883)
Rensselaer	St. Joseph's College Library (1964)
Richmond	Earlham College, Lilly Library (1964)
	Morrison-Reeves Library (1906)
South Bend	Indiana University at South Bend Library (1965)
Terre Haute	Indiana State University, Cunningham Memorial Library (1906)
Valparaiso	Valparaiso University, Moellering Memorial Library (1930)

IOWA

Ames	Iowa State University of Science and Technology Library (1907)

Cedar Falls	University of Northern Iowa Library (1946)
Council Bluffs	Free Public Library (1885)
	Iowa Western Community College, Hoover Media Library (1972)
Davenport	Davenport Public Library (1973)
Des Moines	Drake University, Cowles Library (1966)
	Drake University Law Library (1972)
	Public Library of Des Moines (1888)
	State Library Commission of Iowa (unknown)
Dubuque	Carnegie-Stout Public Library (unknown)
	Loras College, Wahlert Memorial Library (1967)
Fayette	Upper Iowa University, Henderson-Wilder Library (1974)
Grinnell	Grinnell College, Burling Library (1874)
Iowa City	University of Iowa, Law Library (1968)
	University of Iowa Library (1884)—regional
Lamoni	Graceland College, Frederick Madison Smith Library (1927)
Mason City	North Iowa Area Community College Library (1976)
Mount Vernon	Cornell College, Russell D. Cole Library (1896)
Orange City	Northwestern College, Ramaker Library (1970)
Sioux City	Sioux City Public Library (1894)

KANSAS

Atchison	Benedictine College Library (1965)
Baldwin City	Baker University Library (1908)
Colby	Colby Community Junior College Library (1968)
Emporia	Kansas State College, William Allen White Library (1909)
Hays	Fort Hays Kansas State College, Forsyth Library (1926)

Hutchinson	Hutchinson Public Library (1963)
Lawrence	University of Kansas, School of Law Library (1971)
	University of Kansas, Watson Library (1869)—regional
Manhattan	Kansas State University, Farrell Library (1907)
Pittsburg	Kansas State College of Pittsburg, Porter Library (1952)
Salina	Kansas Wesleyan University, Memorial Library (1930)
Topeka	Kansas State Historical Society Library (1877)
	Kansas State Library (unknown)
	Kansas Supreme Court Law Library (1975)
	Washburn University of Topeka, Law Library (1971)
Wichita	Wichita State University Library (1901)

KENTUCKY

Ashland	Ashland Public Library (1946)
Barbourville	Union College, Abigail E. Weeks Memorial Library (1958)
Bowling Green	Western Kentucky University, Cravens Graduate Center and Library (1934)
Danville	Centre College of Kentucky, Grace Doherty Library (1884)
Fort Mitchell	Thomas More College Library (1970)
Frankfort	Kentucky Department of Libraries (1967)
	Kentucky State University, Blazer Library (1972)
	State Law Library (unknown)
Highland Heights	Northern Kentucky University, W. Frank Steely Library (1973)
Hopkinsville	Hopkinsville Community College Library (1976)
Lexington	University of Kentucky Law Library (1968)
	University of Kentucky, Margaret I. King Library (1907)—regional

Louisville	Louisville Free Public Library (1904)
	University of Louisville, Belknap Campus Library (1925)
	University of Louisville, Law Library (1975)
Morehead	Morehead State University, Johnson Camden Library (1955)
Murray	Murray State University Library (1966)
Owensboro	Kentucky Wesleyan College Library (1966)
Richmond	Eastern Kentucky University, John Grant Crabbe Library (1966)

LOUISIANA

Baton Rouge	Louisiana State Library (1976)
	Louisiana State University Law Library (1929)
	Louisiana State University Library (1907)—regional
	Southern University Library (1952)
Eunice	Louisiana State University at Eunice, Le Doux Library (unknown)
Hammond	Southeastern Louisiana University, Sims Memorial Library (1966)
Lafayette	University of Southwestern Louisiana Library (1938)
Lake Charles	McNeese State University, Frazar Memorial Library (1941)
Monroe	Northeast Louisiana University, Sandel Library (1963)
Natchitoches	Northwestern State University, Watson Memorial Library (1887)
New Orleans	Isaac Delgado College, Moss Technical Library (1968)
	Law Library of Louisiana (unknown)
	Loyola University Library (1942)
	New Orleans Public Library (1883)
	Southern University in New Orleans Library (1962)
	Tulane University, Howard-Tilton Memorial Library (1942)

Tulane University Law Library (1976)
U. S. Court of Appeals, Fifth Circuit
   Library (1973)
University of New Orleans Library
   (1963)

Pineville   Louisiana College, Richard W. Norton
   Memorial Library (1969)

Ruston   Louisiana Technical University Library
   (1896)—regional

Shreveport   Louisiana State University at
   Shreveport Library (1967)
Shreve Memorial Library (1923)

Thibodaux   Francis T. Nicholls State University,
   Leonidas Polk Library (1962)

MAINE

Augusta   Maine Law and Legislative Reference
   Library (1973)
Maine State Library (unknown)

Bangor   Bangor Public Library (1884)

Brunswick   Bowdoin College,
   Hawthorne-Longfellow Library
   (1884)

Castine   Maine Maritime Academy, Nutting
   Memorial Library (1969)

Lewiston   Bates College Library (1882)

Orono   University of Maine at Orono,
   Raymond H. Folger Library
   (1907)—regional

Portland   Portland Public Library (1884)
University of Maine Law Library
   (1964)

Springvale   Nasson College Library (1961)

Waterville   Colby College Library (1884)

MARYLAND

Annapolis   Maryland State Library (unknown)
U. S. Naval Academy, Nimitz Library
   (1895)

Baltimore   Enoch Pratt Free Library (1887)
Johns Hopkins University, Milton S.
   Eisenhower Library (1882)

	Morgan State College, Soper Library (1940)
	University of Baltimore, Langsdale Library (1973)
	University of Maryland, Baltimore County Library (1971)
	University of Maryland, School of Law Library (1969)
Bel Air	Harford Community College Library (1967)
Beltsville	Department of Agriculture, National Agricultural Library (1895)
Chestertown	Washington College, Chester M. Miller Library (1891)
College Park	University of Maryland, McKeldin Library (1925)—regional
Cumberland	Allegany Community College Library (1974)
Frostburg	Frostburg State College Library (1967)
Germantown	Energy Research and Development Administration Library (1963)
Patuxent River	Naval Air Station Library (1968)
Rockville	Montgomery County Department of Public Libraries (1951)
Salisbury	Salisbury State College, Blackwell Library (1965)
Towson	Goucher College, Julia Rogers Library (1966)
Westminster	Western Maryland College Library (1896)

MASSACHUSETTS

Amherst	Amherst College Library (1884)
	University of Massachusetts, Godell Library (1907)
Belmont	Belmont Memorial Library (1968)
Boston	Boston Athenaeum Library (unknown)
	Boston College, Bapst Library (1963)
	Boston Public Library (1859)—regional
	Northeastern University, Dodge Library (1962)

	State Library of Massachusetts (unknown)
Brookline	Public Library of Brookline (1925)
Cambridge	Harvard College Library (1860)
	Massachusetts Institute of Technology Libraries (1946)
Chicopee	Our Lady of the Elms College Library (1969)
Lowell	Lowell Technological Institute, Alumni Memorial Library (1952)
Lynn	Lynn Public Library (1953)
Marlborough	Marlborough Public Library (1971)
Medford	Tufts University Library (1899)
Milton	Curry College Library (1972)
New Bedford	New Bedford Free Public Library (1858)
North Dartmouth	Southeastern Massachusetts University Library (1965)
North Easton	Stonehill College, Cushing-Martin Library (1962)
Springfield	Springfield City Library (1966)
Waltham	Brandeis University, Goldfarb Library (1965)
Wellesley	Wellesley College Library (1943)
Wenham	Gordon College, Winn Library (1963)
Williamstown	Williams College Library (unknown)
Worcester	American Antiquarian Society Library (1814)
	University of Massachusetts, Medical Center Library (1972)
	Worcester Public Library (1859)

MICHIGAN

Albion	Albion College, Stockwell Memorial Library (1966)
Allendale	Grand Valley State College Library (1963)
Alma	Alma College, Monteith Library (1963)
Ann Arbor	Great Lakes Basin Commission Library (1971)
	University of Michigan, Harlan Hatcher Library (1884)

127

Benton Harbor	Benton Harbor Public Library (1907)
Bloomfield Hills	Cranbrook Institute of Science Library (1940)
Dearborn	Henry Ford Centennial Library (1969)
	Henry Ford Community College Library (1957)
Detroit	Detroit Public Library (1868)—regional
	Marygrove College Library (1965)
	Mercy College of Detroit Library (1965)
	University of Detroit Library (1884)
	Wayne State University, G. Flint Purdy Library (1973)
	Wayne State University Law Library (1971)
Dowagiac	Southwestern Michigan College Library (1971)
East Lansing	Michigan State University, Law Library (1971)
	Michigan State University Library (1907)
Escanaba	Michigan State Library, Upper Peninsula Branch (1964)
Farmington	Martin Luther King Learning Resources Center, Oakland Community College (1968)
Flint	Charles Stewart Mott Library (1959)
	Flint Public Library (1967)
Grand Rapids	Calvin College Library (1967)
	Grand Rapids Public Library (1876)
Houghton	Michigan Technological University Library (1876)
Jackson	Jackson Public Library (1965)
Kalamazoo	Kalamazoo Library System (1907)
	Western Michigan University, Dwight B. Waldo Library (1963)
Lansing	Michigan State Library (unknown)—regional
Livonia	Schoolcraft College Library (1962)
Marquette	Northern Michigan University, Olsen Library (1963)
Monroe	Monroe County Library System (1974)

Mt. Clemens	Macomb County Library (1968)
Mt. Pleasant	Central Michigan University Library (1958)
Muskegon	Hackley Public Library (1894)
Olivet	Olivet College Library (1974)
Petoskey	North Central Michigan College Library (1962)
Port Huron	Saint Clair County Library System (1876)
Rochester	Oakland University, Kresge Library (1964)
Sagina	Hoyt Public Library (1890)
Traverse City	Northwestern Michigan College, Mark Osterlin Library (1964)
University Center	Delta College Library (1963)
Warren	Warren Public Library, Arthur J. Miller Branch (1973)
Wayne	Wayne Oakland Federated Library System (1957)
Ypsilanti	Eastern Michigan University Library (1965)

MINNESOTA

Bemidji	Bemidji State College, A. C. Clark Library (1963)
Collegeville	St. John's University, Alcuin Library (1954)
Duluth	Duluth Public Library (1909)
Mankato	Mankato State College Memorial Library (1962)
Minneapolis	Anoka County Library (1971)
	Hennepin County Libraries (1971)
	Minneapolis Public Library (1893)
	University of Minnesota, Wilson Library (1907)—regional
Moorhead	Moorhead State College Library (1956)
Morris	University of Minnesota, Morris, Library (1963)
Northfield	Carleton College Library (1930)
	St. Olaf College, Rolvaag Memorial Library (1930)

129

St. Cloud	St. Cloud State College Library (1962)
St. Paul	Minnesota Historical Society Library (1867)
	Minnesota State Law Library (unknown)
	St. Paul Public Library (1914)
	University of Minnesota, St. Paul Campus Library (1974)
St. Peter	Gustavus Adolphus College Library (1941)
Stillwater	Stillwater Public Library (1893)
Willmar	Crow River Regional Library (1958)
Winona	Winona State University, Maxwell Library (1969)

MISSISSIPPI

Cleveland	Delta State University, W. B. Roberts Library (1975)
Clinton	Mississippi College School of Law Library (1977)
Columbus	Mississsippi State College for Women, J. C. Fant Memorial Library (1920)
Hattiesburg	University of Southern Mississippi Library (1935)
Jackson	Jackson State College Library (1968)
	Millsaps College, Millsaps-Wilson Library (1963)
	Mississippi Library Commission (1947)
	Mississippi State Law Library (unknown)
Lorman	Alcorn Agricultural and Mechanical College Library (1970)
State College	Mississippi State University, Mitchell Memorial Library (1907)
University	University of Mississippi Library (1833)—regional
	University of Mississippi, School of Law Library (1967)

MISSOURI

| Cape Girardeau | Southeast Missouri State College, Kent Library (1916) |

Columbia	University of Missouri Library (1862)
Fayette	Central Methodist College Library (1962)
Fulton	Westminster College, Reeves Library (1875)
Jefferson City	Lincoln University, Inman E. Page Library (1944)
	Missouri State Library (1963)
	Missouri Supreme Court Library (unknown)
Joplin	Missouri Southern State College Library (1966)
Kansas City	Kansas City Public Library (1881)
	Rockhurst College Library (1917)
	University of Missouri at Kansas City, General Library (1938)
Kirksville	Northeast Missouri State Teachers College, Pickler Memorial Library (1966)
Liberty	William Jewell College Library (1900)
Rolla	University of Missouri at Rolla Library (1907)
St. Charles	Lindenwood College, Margaret Leggat Butler Library (1973)
St. Joseph	Maryville College of the Sacred Heart Library (1976)
	St. Joseph Public Library (1891)
St. Louis	St. Louis County Library (1970)
	St. Louis Public Library (1866)
	St. Louis University, Law Library (1967)
	St. Louis University, Pius XII Memorial Library (1866)
	U. S. Court of Appeals, Eighth Circuit Library (1972)
	University of Missouri at St. Louis, Thomas Jefferson Library (1966)
	Washington University, John M. Olin Library (1906)
Springfield	Drury College, Walker Library (1874)
	Southwest Missouri State College, Library (1963)

Warrensburg	Central Missouri State College, Ward Edwards Library (1914)

MONTANA

Billings	Eastern Montana College Library (1924)
Bozeman	Montana State University Library (1907)
Butte	Montana College of Mineral Science and Technology Library (1901)
Helena	Carroll College Library (1974)
	Montana Historical Society Library (unknown)
	Montana State Library (1966)
	State Law Library of Montana (1977)
Missoula	University of Montana Library (1909)—regional

NEBRASKA

Blair	Dana College, Dana-LIFE Library (1924)
Crete	Doane College, Whitin Library (1944)
Fremont	Midland Lutheran College Library (1924)
Kearney	Kearney State College, Calvin T. Ryan Library (1962)
Lincoln	Nebraska Publications Clearinghouse, Nebraska Library Commission (unknown)—regional
	Nebraska State Library (unknown)
	University of Nebraska, Con. L. Love Memorial Library (1907)
Omaha	Creighton University, Alumni Library (1924)
	Omaha Public Library (1880)
	University of Nebraska at Omaha, University Library (1939)
Scottsbluff	Scottsbluff Public Library (1925)
Wayne	Wayne State College, U. S. Conn Library (1970)

NEVADA

Carson City	Nevada State Library (unknown)
	Nevada Supreme Court Library (1973)
Las Vegas	Clark County Library, District Library (1974)
	University of Nevada at Las Vegas, James R. Dickinson Library (1959)
Reno	Nevada State Historical Society Library (1974)
	University of Nevada Library (1970)—regional

NEW HAMPSHIRE

Concord	Franklin Pierce Law Center Library (1973)
	New Hampshire State Library (unknown)
Durham	University of New Hampshire Library (1907)
Franconia	Franconia College Library (1972)
Hanover	Dartmouth College, Baker Library (1884)
Henniker	New England College Library (1966)
Manchester	Manchester City Library (1966)
	New Hampshire College, H. A. B. Shapiro Memorial Library (1976)
	St. Anselm's College, Geise Library (1963)
Nashua	Nashua Public Library (1971)

NEW JERSEY

Bayonne	Bayonne Free Public Library (1909)
Bloomfield	Free Public Library of Bloomfield (1965)
Bridgeton	Cumberland County Library (1966)
Camden	Rutgers University-Camden Library (1966)
Convent Station	College of St. Elizabeth, Mahoney Library (1938)
Dover	County College of Morris Library, Learning Resources Center (1975)

East Brunswick	East Brunswick Public Library (1977)
East Orange	East Orange Public Library (1966)
Elizabeth	Free Public Library of Elizabeth (1895)
Glassboro	Glassboro State College, Savitz Learning Resource Center (1963)
Hackensack	Johnson Free Public Library (1966)
Irvington	Free Public Library of Irvington (1966)
Jersey City	Free Public Library of Jersey City (1879)
	Jersey City State College, Forrest A. Irwin Library (1963)
Lawrenceville	Rider College Library (1975)
Madison	Drew University, Rose Memorial Library (1939)
Mahwah	Ramapo College Library (1971)
Mount Holly	Burlington County Library (1966)
New Brunswick	Free Public Library (1908)
	Rutgers University Library (1907)
Newark	Newark Public Library (1906)—regional
	Rutgers-The State University, John Cotton Dana Library (1966)
Passaic	Passaic Public Library (1964)
Phillipsburg	Phillipsburg Free Public Library (1976)
Plainfield	Plainfield Public Library (1971)
Pomona	Stockton State College Library (1972)
Princeton	Princeton University Library (1884)
Rutherford	Fairleigh Dickinson University, Messler Library (1953)
Shrewsbury	Monmouth County Library (1968)
South Orange	Seton Hall University Library (1947)
Teaneck	Fairleigh Dickinson University, Teaneck Campus Library (1963)
Toms River	Ocean County College Learning Resources Center (1966)
Trenton	New Jersey State Library, Law and Reference Bureau, Department of Education (unknown)
	Trenton Free Public Library (1902)
Union	Kean College of New Jersey, Nancy Thompson Library (1973)

Upper Montclair   Montclair State College, Harry A.
      Sprague Library (1967)
Wayne   Wayne Public Library (1972)
West Long Branch   Monmouth College, Guggenheim
      Memorial Library (1963)
Woodbridge   Free Public Library of Woodbridge
      (1965)

NEW MEXICO
Albuquerque   University of New Mexico, Medical
      Sciences Library (1973)
      University of New Mexico, School of
      Law Library (1973)
      University of New Mexico, Zimmerman
      Library (1896)—regional
Hobbs   New Mexico Junior College, Pannell
      Library (1969)
Las Cruces   New Mexico State University Library
      (1907)
Las Vegas   New Mexico Highlands University,
      Donnelly Library (1913)
Portales   Eastern New Mexico University
      Library (1962)
Santa Fe   New Mexico State Library
      (1960)—regional
      Supreme Court Law Library
      (unknown)
Silver City   Western New Mexico University, Miller
      Library (1972)

NEW YORK
Albany   New York State Library
      (unknown)—regional
      State University of New York at
      Albany Library (1964)
Auburn   Seymour Library (1972)
Bayside   Queensborough Community College
      Library (1972)
Binghamton   State University of New York at
      Binghamton Library (1962)

Brockport	State University of New York, Drake Memorial Library (1967)
Bronx	Herbert H. Lehman College Library (1967)
	New York Public Library, Mott Haven Branch (1973)
Bronxville	Sarah Lawrence College Library (1969)
Brooklyn	Brooklyn College Library (1936)
	Brooklyn Law School, Law Library (1974)
	Brooklyn Public Library (1908)
	Polytechnic Institute of Brooklyn, Spicer Library (1963)
	Pratt Institute Library (1891)
	State University of New York, Downstate Medical Center Library (1958)
Buffalo	Buffalo and Erie County Public Library (1895)
	State University of New York at Buffalo, Lockwood Memorial Library (1963)
Canton	St. Lawrence University, Owen D. Young Library (1920)
Corning	Corning Community College, Arthur A. Houghton, Jr. Library (1963)
Cortland	State University of New York College at Cortland, Memorial Library (1964)
Delhi	State University Agricultural and Technical College Library (1970)
Douglaston	Cathedral College of the Immaculate Conception Library (1971)
East Islip	East Islip Public Library (1974)
Elmira	Elmira College, Gannett-Tripp Learning Center (1956)
Farmingdale	State University Agricultural and Technical Institute at Farmingdale Library (1917)
Flushing	Queens College, Paul Klapper Library (1939)

Garden City	Adelphi University, Swirbul Library (1966)
	Nassau Library System (1965)
Geneseo	State University College, Milne Library (1967)
Greenvale	C. W. Post College, B. Davis Schwartz Memorial Library (1965)
Hamilton	Colgate University Library (1902)
Hempstead	Hofstra University Library (1964)
Ithaca	Cornell University Library (1907)
	New York State Colleges of Agriculture and Home Economics, Albert R. Mann Library (1943)
Jamaica	Queens Borough Public Library (1926)
	St. John's University Library (1956)
Kings Point	U. S. Merchant Marine Academy Library (1962)
Mount Vernon	Mount Vernon Public Library (1962)
New Paltz	State University College Library (1965)
New York City	City University of New York, City College Library (1884)
	College of Insurance, Ecker Library (1965)
	Columbia University Libraries (1882)
	Cooper Union Library (1930)
	Fordham University Library (1937)
	Medical Library Center of New York (1976)
	New York Law Institute Library (1909)
	New York Public Library (Astor Branch) (1907)
	New York Public Library (Lenox Branch) (1884)
	New York University, Law Library (1973)
	New York University Libraries (1967)
	State University of New York, Maritime College Library (1947)
	U. S. Court of Appeals Library (1976)
Newburgh	Newburgh Free Library (1909)

Niagara Falls	Niagara Falls Public Library (1976)
Oakdale	Dowling College Library (1965)
Oneonta	State University College, James M. Milne Library (1966)
Oswego	State University College, Penfield Library (1966)
Plattsburgh	State University College, Benjamin F. Feinberg Library (1967)
Potsdam	Clarkson College of Technology, Harriet Call Burnap Memorial Library (1938)
	State University College, Frederick W. Crumb Memorial Library (1964)
Poughkeepsie	Vassar College Library (1943)
Purchase	State University of New York, College at Purchase Library (1969)
Rochester	Rochester Public Library (1963)
	University of Rochester Library (1880)
St. Bonaventure	St. Bonaventure College, Friedsam Memorial Library (1938)
Saratoga Springs	Skidmore College Library (1964)
Schenectady	Union College, Schaffer Library (1901)
Southampton	Southampton College Library (1973)
Staten Island (Grymes Hill)	Wagner College, Horrmann Library (1953)
Stony Brook	State University of New York at Stony Brook Library (1963)
Syracuse	Syracuse University Library (1878)
Troy	Troy Public Library (1869)
Utica	Utica Public Library (1885)
	Utica/Rome State University College Library (1977)
West Point	U. S. Military Academy Library (unknown)
Yonkers	Yonkers Public Library (1910)
Yorktown Heights	Mercy College at Fox Meadow Library (1976)

NORTH CAROLINA

Asheville	University of North Carolina at Asheville, D. Hiden Ramsey Library (1965)

Boiling Springs	Gardner-Webb College, Dover Memorial Library (1974)
Boone	Appalachian State University Library (1963)
Buies Creek	Campbell College, Carrie Rich Memorial Library (1965)
Chapel Hill	University of North Carolina at Chapel Hill Library (1884)—regional
Charlotte	Public Library of Charlotte and Mecklenburg County (1964)
	Queens College, Everette Library (1927)
	University of North Carolina at Charlotte, Atkins Library (1964)
Cullowhee	Western Carolina University, Hunter Library (1953)
Davidson	Davidson College, Hugh A. and Jane Grey Memorial Library (1893)
Durham	Duke University, William R. Perkins Library (1890)
	North Carolina Central University, James E. Shepard Memorial Library (1973)
Elon College	Elon College Library (1971)
Fayetteville	Fayetteville State University, Chesnutt Library (1971)
Greensboro	North Carolina Agricultural and Technical State University, F. D. Bluford Library (1937)
	University of North Carolina at Greensboro, Walter Clinton Jackson Library (1963)
Greenville	East Carolina University, J. Y. Joyner Library (1951)
Laurinburg	St. Andrews Presbyterian College, DeTamble Library (1969)
Lexington	Davidson County Public Library System (1971)
Mount Olive	Mount Olive College, Moye Library (1971)
Murfreesboro	Chowan College, Whitaker Library (1963)

139

Pembroke	Pembroke State University, Mary Livermore Library (1965)
Raleigh	North Carolina State Library (unknown)
	North Carolina State University, D. H. Hill Library (1923)
	North Carolina Supreme Court Library (1972)
	Wake County Public Libraries (1969)
Rocky Mount	North Carolina Wesleyan College Library (1969)
Salisbury	Catawba College Library (1925)
Wilmington	University of North Carolina at Wilmington, William M. Randall Library (1965)
Wilson	Atlantic Christian College, Clarence L. Hardy Library (1930)
Winston-Salem	Forsyth County Public Library System (1954)
	Wake Forest University, Z. Smith Reynolds Library (1902)

NORTH DAKOTA

Bismarck	North Dakota State Law Library (unknown)
	State Historical Society of North Dakota (1907)
	State Library Commission Library (1971)
	Veterans Memorial Public Library (1967)
Dickinson	Dickinson State College Library (1968)
Fargo	Fargo Public Library (1964)
	North Dakota State University Library (1907)—regional, in cooperation with University of North Dakota, Chester Fritz Library (1890)
Grand Forks	University of North Dakota, Chester Fritz Library at Grand Forks (unknown)

Minot	Minot State College, Memorial Library (1925)
Valley City	State College Library (1913)

OHIO

Ada	Ohio Northern University, J. P. Taggart Law Library (1965)
Akron	Akron Public Library (1952)
	University of Akron Library (1963)
Alliance	Mount Union College Library (1888)
Ashland	Ashland College Library (1938)
Athens	Ohio University Library (1886)
Batavia	Clermont General and Technical College Library (1973)
Bluffton	Bluffton College, Musselman Library (1951)
Bowling Green	Bowling Green State University Library (1933)
Canton	Malone College, Everett L. Cattell Library (1970)
Chardon	Geauga County Public Library (1971)
Cincinnati	Public Library of Cincinnati and Hamilton County (1884)
	University of Cincinnati Library (1929)
Cleveland	Case Western Reserve University, Freiberger Library (1913)
	Cleveland Heights-University Heights Public Library (1970)
	Cleveland Public Library (1886)
	Cleveland State University Library (1966)
	John Carroll University, Grasselli Library (1963)
	Municipal Reference Library (1970)
Columbus	Capital University Library (1968)
	Ohio State Library (unknown)—regional
	Ohio State University Library (1907)
	Ohio Supreme Court Law Library (1973)

141

	Public Library of Columbus and Franklin County (1885)
Dayton	Dayton and Montgomery County Public Library (1909)
	University of Dayton, Albert Emanuel Library (1969)
	Wright State University, Library (1965)
Delaware	Ohio Wesleyan University, L. A. Beeghly Library (1845)
Elyria	Elyria Public Library (1966)
Findlay	Findlay College, Shafer Library (1969)
Gambier	Kenyon College, Library (1873)
Granville	Denison University Library (1884)
Hiram	Hiram College, Teachout-Price Memorial Library (1874)
Kent	Kent State University Library (1962)
Marietta	Marietta College, Dawes Memorial Library (1884)
Middletown	Miami University at Middletown, Gardner-Harvey Library (1970)
New Concord	Muskingum College Library (1966)
Oberlin	Oberlin College Library (1858)
Oxford	Miami University, Alumni Library (1909)
Portsmouth	Portsmouth Public Library (unknown)
Rio Grande	Rio Grande College, Jeanette Albiez Davis Library (1966)
Springfield	Warder Public Library (1884)
Steubenville	College of Steubenville, Starvaggi Memorial Library (1971)
	Public Library of Steubenville and Jefferson County (1950)
Tiffin	Heidelberg College, Beeghly Library (1964)
Toledo	Toledo-Lucas County Public Library (1884)
	University of Toledo Library (1963)
Westerville	Otterbein College, Centennial Library (1967)
Wooster	College of Wooster, Andrews Library (1966)

Youngstown	Public Library of Youngstown and Mahoning County (1923)
	Youngstown State University, William F. Maag Library (1971)

OKLAHOMA

Ada	East Central State College, Linscheid Library (1914)
Alva	Northwestern State College Library (1907)
Bartlesville	United States ERDA-BERC Library (1962)
Bethany	Bethany Nazarene College, R. T. Williams Library (1971)
Durant	Southeastern State College Library (1929)
Edmond	Central State University Library (1934)
Enid	Public Library of Enid and Garfield County (1908)
Langston	Langston University, G. Lamar Harrison Library (1941)
Muskogee	Muskogee Public Library (1971)
Norman	University of Oklahoma Libraries (1893)
Oklahoma City	Oklahoma County Libraries (1974)
	Oklahoma City University Library (1963)
	Oklahoma Department of Libraries (1893)—regional
Shawnee	Oklahoma Baptist University Library (1933)
Stillwater	Oklahoma State University Library (1907)
Tahlequah	Northeastern State College, John Vaughan Library (1923)
Tulsa	Tulsa City-County Library Commission (1963)
	University of Tulsa, McFarlin Library (1929)

143

Weatherford	Southwestern Oklahoma State University, Al Harris Library (1958)

OREGON

Ashland	Southern Oregon College Library (1953)
Corvallis	Oregon State University Library (1907)
Eugene	University of Oregon Library (1883)
Forest Grove	Pacific University Library (1897)
La Grande	Eastern Oregon College, Walter M. Pierce Library (1954)
McMinnville	Linfield College, Northup Library (1965)
Monmouth	Oregon College of Education Library (1967)
Portland	Department of the Interior, Bonneville Power Administration Library (1962)
	Lewis and Clark College, Aubrey R. Watzek Library (1967)
	Library Association of Portland (1884)
	Portland State University Library (1963)—regional
	Reed College Library (1912)
Salem	Oregon State Library (unknown)
	Oregon Supreme Court Library (1974)
	Williamette University Library (1969)

PENNSYLVANIA

Allentown	Muhlenberg College, Haas Library (1939)
Altoona	Altoona Public Library (1969)
Bethlehem	Lehigh University, Linderman Library (1876)
Blue Bell	Montgomery County Community College, Learning Resources Center Library (1975)
Carlisle	Dickinson College, Boyd Lee Spahr Library (1947)
Cheyney	Cheyney State College, Leslie Pickney Hill Library (1947)
Collegeville	Ursinus College, Myrin Library (1963)

Doylestown	Bucks County Free Library, Center County Library (1970)
East Stroudsburg	East Stroudsburg State College, Kemp Library (1966)
Erie	Erie Public Library (1897)
Greenville	Thiel College, Langenheim Memorial Library (1963)
Harrisburg	State Library of Pennsylvania (unknown)—regional
Haverford	Haverford College Library (1897)
Hazleton	Hazleton Area Public Library (1964)
Indiana	Indiana University of Pennsylvania, Rhodes R. Stabley Library (1962)
Johnstown	Cambria Public Library (1965)
Lancaster	Franklin and Marshall College, Fackenthal Library (1895)
Lewisburg	Bucknell University, Ellen Clarke Bertrand Library (1963)
Mansfield	Mansfield State College Library (1968)
Meadville	Allegheny College, Reis Library (1907)
Millersville	Millersville State College, Ganser Library (1966)
Monessen	Monessen Public Library (1969)
New Castle	New Castle Free Public Library (1963)
Newtown	Bucks County Community College Library (1968)
Norristown	Montgomery County-Norristown Public Library (1969)
Philadelphia	Drexel University Library (1963)
	Free Library of Philadelphia (1897)
	St. Joseph's College Library (1974)
	Temple University, Samuel Paley Library (1947)
	U. S. Court of Appeals, Third Circuit (1973)
	University of Pennsylvania, Biddle Law Library (1974)
	University of Pennsylvania Library (1886)
Pittsburgh	Bureau of Mines, Pittsburgh Research Center Library (1962)

145

	Carnegie Library of Pittsburgh (1895)
	Carnegie Library of Pittsburgh, Allegheny Regional Branch (1924)
	La Roche College, John J. Wright Library (1974)
	University of Pittsburgh, Hillman Library (1910)
Pottsville	Pottsville Free Public Library (1967)
Reading	Reading Public Library (1901)
Scranton	Scranton Public Library (1895)
Shippensburg	Shippensburg State College, Ezra Lehman Memorial Library (1973)
Slippery Rock	Slippery Rock State College, Maltby Library (1965)
Swarthmore	Swarthmore College Library (1923)
University Park	Pennsylvania State University Library (1907)
Villanova	Villanova University, School of Law Library (1964)
Warren	Warren Library Association, Warren Public Library (1885)
Washington	Washington and Jefferson College, Memorial Library (1884)
Waynesburg	Waynesburg College Library (1964)
West Chester	West Chester State College, Francis Harvey Green Library (1967)
Wilkes-Barre	King's College, D. Leonard Corgan Library (1949)
Williamsport	Lycoming College Library (1970)
York	York Junior College Library (1963)
Youngwood	Westmoreland County Community College, Learning Resource Center (1972)

PUERTO RICO

Mayaguez	University of Puerto Rico, Mayaguez Campus Library (1928)
Ponce	Catholic University of Puerto Rico Library (1966)
Rio Piedras	University of Puerto Rico General Library (1928)

RHODE ISLAND

Kingston	University of Rhode Island Library (1907)
Newport	Naval War College Library (1963)
Providence	Brown University, John D. Rockefeller Jr., Library (unknown)
	Providence College, Phillips Memorial Library (1969)
	Providence Public Library (1884)
	Rhode Island College Library (1965)
	Rhode Island State Library (before 1895)
Warwick	Warwick Public Library (1966)
Westerly	Westerly Public Library (1909)
Woonsocket	Woonsocket Harris Public Library (1977)

SOUTH CAROLINA

Charleston	Baptist College at Charleston Library (1967)
	The Citadel Memorial Library (1962)
	College of Charleston Library (1869)
Clemson	Clemson University Library (1893)
Columbia	Benedict College, Learning Resources Center (1969)
	South Carolina State Library (before 1895)
	University of South Carolina Undergraduate Library (1884)
Conway	University of South Carolina, Coastal Carolina Regional Campus Library (1974)
Due West	Erskine College, McCain Library (1968)
Florence	Florence County Library (1967)
	Francis Marion College, James A. Rogers Library (1970)
Greenville	Furman University Library (1962)
	Greenville County Library (1966)
Greenwood	Lander College Library (1967)
Orangeburg	South Carolina State College, Whittaker Library (1953)

147

Rock Hill	Winthrop College Library (1896)
Spartanburg	Spartanburg County Public Library (1967)

SOUTH DAKOTA

Aberdeen	Northern State College Library (1963)
Brookings	South Dakota State University, H. M. Briggs Library (1889)
Pierre	South Dakota State Library (1973)
Rapid City	Rapid City Public Library (1963)
	South Dakota School of Mines and Technology Library (1963)
Sioux Falls	Augustana College, Mikkelsen Library and Learning Resources Center (1969)
	Sioux Falls Public Library (1903)
Spearfish	Black Hills State College Library (1942)
Vermillion	University of South Dakota, I. D. Weeks Library (1889)
Yankton	Yankton College, Corliss Lay Library (1904)

TENNESSEE

Bristol	King College Library (1970)
Chattanooga	Chattanooga-Hamilton County Bicentennial Library (1908)
	TVA Technical Library (1976)
Clarksville	Austin Peay State University, Felix G. Woodward Library (1945)
Cleveland	Cleveland State Community College Library (1973)
Columbia	Columbia State Community College Library (1973)
Cookeville	Tennessee Technological University, Jere Whitson Memorial Library (1969)
Jackson	Lambuth College, Luther L. Gobbel Library (1967)
Jefferson City	Carson-Newman College Library (1964)
Johnson City	East Tennessee State University, Sherrod Library (1942)

Knoxville
Public Library of Knoxville and Knox
County, Lawson McGhee Library
(1973)
University of Tennessee at Knoxville
Library (1907)
University of Tennessee Law Library
(1971)

Martin
University of Tennessee at Martin
Library (1957)

Memphis
Memphis and Shelby County Public
Library and Information Center
(1896)
Memphis State University, John W.
Brister Library (1966)

Murfreesboro
Middle Tennessee State University,
Andrew L. Todd Library (1912)

Nashville
Fisk University Library (1965)
Joint University Libraries (1884)
Public Library of Nashville and
Davidson County (1884)
Tennessee State Library and Archives,
State Library Division (unknown)
Tennessee State Supreme Court Law
Library (1976)
Tennessee State University, Martha M.
Brown Memorial Library (1972)
Vanderbilt University Law Library
(1976)

Sewanee
University of the South, Jesse Ball
duPont Library (1873)

TEXAS

Abilene
Hardin-Simmons University Library
(1940)

Arlington
Arlington Public Library (1970)
University of Texas at Arlington
Library (1963)

Austin
Texas State Law Library (1972)
Texas State Library
(unknown)—regional
University of Texas Library (1884)

149

	University of Texas Lyndon B. Johnson School of Public Affairs Library (1966)
	University of Texas, School of Law Library (1965)
Baytown	Lee College Library (1970)
Beaumont	Lamar University Library (1957)
Brownwood	Howard Payne College, Walker Memorial Library (1964)
Canyon	West Texas State University Library (1928)
College Station	Texas Agricultural and Mechanical University Library (1907)
Commerce	East Texas State University Library (1937)
Corpus Christi	Texas Arts and Industries University at Corpus Christi Library (1976)
Corsicana	Navarro Junior College Library (1965)
Dallas	Bishop College, Zale Library (1966)
	Dallas Baptist College Library (1967)
	Dallas Public Library (1900)
	Southern Methodist University, Fondren Library (1925)
	University of Texas Health Science Center Library at Dallas (1975)
Denton	North Texas State University Library (1948)
Edinburg	Pan American University Library (1959)
El Paso	El Paso Public Library (1906)
	University of Texas at El Paso Library (1966)
Fort Worth	Fort Worth Public Library (1905)
	Texas Christian University, Mary Couts Burnett Library (1916)
Galveston	Rosenberg Library (1909)
Houston	Houston Public Library (1884)
	North Harris County College, Learning Resource Center (1974)
	Rice University, Fondren Library (1967)

	University of Houston Library (1957)
Huntsville	Sam Houston State University, Estill Library (1949)
Irving	Irving Municipal Library (1974)
Kingsville	Texas Arts and Industries University Library (1944)
Lake Jackson	Brazosport College Library (1969)
Laredo	Laredo Junior College Library (1970)
Longview	Nicholson Memorial Public Library (1961)
Lubbock	Texas Tech University Library (1962)
Marshall	Wiley College, Cole Library (1962)
Mesquite	Mesquite Public Library (1975)
Nacogdoches	Stephen F. Austin State University, Steen Library (1965)
Plainview	Wayland Baptist College, Van Howeling Memorial Library (1963)
Richardson	University of Texas at Dallas Library (1972)
San Angelo	Angelo State University, Porter Henderson Library (1964)
San Antonio	St. Mary's University Library (1964)
	San Antonio College Library (1972)
	San Antonio Public Library, Business and Science Department (1899)
	Trinity University Library (1964)
	University of Texas at San Antonio Library (1973)
San Marcos	Southwest Texas State University Library (1955)
Seguin	Texas Lutheran College, Blumberg Memorial Library (1970)
Sherman	Austin College, Arthur Hopkins Library (1963)
Texarkana	Texarkana Community College, Palmer Memorial Library (1963)
Victoria	University of Houston, Victoria Campus Library (1973)
Waco	Baylor University Library (1905)
Wichita Falls	Midwestern University, Moffett Library (1963)

151

UTAH

Cedar City	Southern Utah State College Library (1964)
Ephraim	Snow College, Lucy A. Phillips Library (1963)
Logan	Utah State University, Merrill Library and Learning Resources Center (1907)—regional
Ogden	Weber State College Library (1962)
Provo	Brigham Young University, Law Library (1972)
	Brigham Young University, Lee Library (1908)
Salt Lake City	University of Utah, Spencer S. Eccles Medical Sciences Library (1970)
	University of Utah, Marriott Library (1893)
	Utah State Library Commission, Documents Library (unknown)
	Utah State Supreme Court Law Library (1975)

VERMONT

Burlington	University of Vermont, Bailey Library (1907)
Castleton	Castleton State College, Calvin Coolidge Library (1969)
Johnson	Johnson State College, John Dewey Library (1955)
Lyndonville	Lyndon State College, Samuel Reed Hall Library (1969)
Middlebury	Middlebury College, Egbert Starr Library (1884)
Montpelier	Vermont Department of Libraries (before 1895)
Northfield	Norwich University Library (1908)
Putney	Windham College, Dorothy Culbertson Marvin Memorial Library (1965)

VIRGIN ISLANDS

Charlotte Amalie	College of the Virgin Islands, Ralph M. Palewonsky Library (1973)

(St. Thomas)	St. Thomas Public Library (1968)
Christiansted	Christiansted Public Library (1974)
(St. Croix)	

VIRGINIA

Blacksburg	Virginia Polytechnic Institute and State University, Newman Library (1907)
Bridgewater	Bridgewater College, Alexander Mark Memorial Library (1902)
Charlottesville	University of Virginia, Alderman Library (1910)—regional
	University of Virginia Law Library (1964)
Chesapeake	Chesapeake Public Library System (1970)
Danville	Danville Community College Library (1969)
Emory	Emory and Henry College Library (1884)
Fairfax	George Mason College of the University of Virginia, Fenwick Library (1960)
Fredericksburg	Mary Washington College, E. Lee Trinkle Library (1940)
Hampden-Sydney	Hampden-Sydney College, Eggleston Library (1891)
Hampton	Hampton Institute, Huntington Memorial Library (1977)
Harrisonburg	James Madison University, Madison Memorial Library (1973)
Hollins College	Hollins College, Fishburn Library (1967)
Lexington	Virginia Military Institute, Preston Library (1874)
	Washington and Lee University, Cyrus Hall McCormick Library (1910)
Martinsville	Patrick Henry Community College Library (1971)
Norfolk	Armed Forces Staff College Library (1963)
	Norfolk Public Library (1895)

153

	Old Dominion University Library (1963)
Petersburg	Virginia State College, Johnston Memorial Library (1907)
Quantico	Federal Bureau of Investigation Academy Library (1970)
	Marine Corps Schools, James Carson Breckinridge Library (1967)
Reston	Department of the Interior, Geological Survey Library (1962)
Richmond	State Law Library (1973)
	U. S. Court of Appeals, Fourth Circuit Library (1973)
	University of Richmond, Boatwright Memorial Library (1900)
	Virginia Commonwealth University, James Branch Cabell Library (1971)
	Virginia State Library (unknown)
Roanoke	Roanoke Public Library (1964)
Salem	Roanoke College Library (1886)
Williamsburg	William and Mary College Library (1936)
Wise	Clinch Valley College, John Cook Wylie Library (1971)

WASHINGTON

Bellingham	Western Washington State College, Wilson Library (1963)
Cheney	Eastern Washington State College Library (1966)
Ellensburg	Central Washington State College Library (1962)
Everett	Everett Public Library (1914)
Olympia	Evergreen State College (1972)
	Washington State Library (unknown)—regional
Port Angeles	North Olympic Library System (1965)
Pullman	Washington State University Library (1907)
Seattle	Seattle Public Library (1908)
	University of Washington Library (1890)

	University of Washington, School of Law Library (1969)
Spokane	Spokane Public Library (1910)
Tacoma	Tacoma Public Library (1894)
	University of Puget Sound, Collins Memorial Library (1938)
Vancouver	Fort Vancouver Regional Library (1962)
Walla Walla	Whitman College, Penrose Memorial Library (1890)

WEST VIRGINIA

Athens	Concord College Library (1924)
Bluefield	Bluefield State College Library (1972)
Charleston	Kanawha County Public Library (1952)
	West Virginia College Graduate Studies (1977)
	West Virginia Library Commission (unknown)
Elkins	Davis and Elkins College Library (1913)
Fairmont	Fairmont State College Library (1884)
Glenville	Glenville State College, Robert F. Kidd Library (1966)
Huntington	Marshall University Library (1925)
Institute	West Virginia State College Library (1907)
Morgantown	West Virginia University Library (1907)—regional
Salem	Salem College Library (1921)
Shepherdstown	Shepherd College Library (1971)
Weirton	Mary H. Weir Public Library (1963)

WISCONSIN

Appleton	Lawrence University, Seeley G. Mudd Library (1869)
Beloit	Beloit College Libraries (1888)
Eau Claire	University of Wisconsin, Eau Claire, William D. McIntyre Library (1951)
Fond du Lac	Fond du Lac Public Library (1966)
Green Bay	University of Wisconsin-Green Bay Library (1968)

155

La Crosse	La Crosse Public Library (1883)
	University of Wisconsin-La Crosse, Murphy Library (1965)
Madison	Department of Public Instruction, Division for Library Services, Reference and Loan Library (1965)
	Madison Public Library (1965)
	State Historical Society Library (1870)—regional, in cooperation with University of Wisconsin Memorial Library
	University of Wisconsin-Madison, Memorial Library (1939)
	Wisconsin State Library (unknown)
Milwaukee	Alverno College Library (1971)
	Milwaukee County Law Library (1934)
	Milwaukee Public Library (1861)—regional
	Mount Mary College Library (1964)
	University of Wisconsin-Milwaukee Library (1960)
Oshkosh	University of Wisconsin-Oshkosh, Forrest R. Polk Library (1956)
Platteville	University of Wisconsin-Platteville, Elton S. Karrmann Library (1964)
Racine	Racine Public Library (1898)
River Falls	University of Wisconsin-River Falls, Chalmer Davee Library (1962)
Stevens Point	University of Wisconsin-Stevens Point, Learning Resources Center (1951)
Superior	Superior Public Library (1908)
	University of Wisconsin-Superior, Jim Dan Hill Library (1935)
Waukesha	Waukesha Public Library (1966)
Wausau	Marathon County Public Library (1971)
Whitewater	University of Wisconsin-Whitewater, Harold Andersen Library (1963)

WYOMING

Casper	Natrona County Public Library (1929)
Cheyenne	Wyoming State Library (unknown)—regional

Laramie	University of Wyoming, Coe Library (1907)
Powell	Northwest Community College Library (1967)
Riverton	Central Wyoming College Library (1969)
Rock Springs	Western Wyoming College Library (1969)
Sheridan	Sheridan College, Mary Brown Kooi Library (1963)

Author Index

Agranoff, Robert, 71, 81
Alexander, Herbert E., 81–82
American Enterprise Institute for Public Policy Research, 26, 86, 88
American Institute of Public Opinion, 86, 89
American Library Association, Government Documents Round Table, 95, 98
American Political Science Association, 78
Arcata Microfilm, 30
Associated Press, 30

Barone, Michael, 63
Benton, Mildred, 95
Berelson, Bernard R., 73
Bitner, Harry, 96
Bone, Hugh A., 71
Boyd, Anne Morris, 97

Brightbill, George D., 104
Brock, Clifton, 98
Brownson, Charles B., 63
Buhler, Michaela, 67
Burnham, Walter Dean, 88
Burns, Elizabeth C., 82
Burns, James MacGregor, 6

Cannon, Clarence, 6
Carrollton Press, 39–40, 99
Carter, Phyllis G., 78
Census, Bureau of, 70, 72, 76–79, 88, 90
Center for the American Woman and Politics, 65
Center for California Public Affairs, 30
Center for Political Studies, 73–74
Chamberlin, Hope, 65
Christian Science Monitor, 29

158

Christopher, Maurine, 64
Citizen's Research Foundation, 81–82, 89
Clerk of the House of Representatives, 41, 70, 82, 89
Commerce Clearing House, 32
Commission on the Operation of the Senate, 73
Common Cause, 83–84, 89
Congress Project (Ralph Nader Congress Project), 65
Congressional Budget Office, 58, 89
Congressional Information Service, 20, 39, 78, 90, 95, 99
Congressional Quarterly, 5, 23–25, 68–69, 77, 81, 84, 90, 93
Congressional Research Service, 33
Consolidated Directories, 67
Council of State Governments, 28, 88
Cox, Edward Franklin, 69, 75
Cronin, Thomas E., 6
Cummings, Frank, 5, 75
Cummings, Milton C., Jr., 6, 75

David, Paul T., 76
Davidson, Roger, 73
DIALOG, 28

Eastin, Roy B., 97
Engelbarts, Rudolf, 63

Federal Communications Commission, 85, 91
Federal Election Commission, 84, 91
Federal Register, Office of, 35
Field, Rochelle, 41
Fischer, Joseph, 5
Folsom, Gwendolyn B., 96
Freides, Thelma, 98

Gallup, George H., 86
Gandet, Hazel, 73
Garrison, Lloyd W., 72
General Accounting Office, 57–58, 91

Goldman, Perry, 66
Government Affairs Institute, 70, 91
Government Research Corporation, 26
Government Documents Round Table, American Library Association, 95, 98

Halvarson, Gary, 41
Harvard Law Review Association, 102
Health, Education and Welfare, Department of, 57, 102
Hinds, Asher C., 6
Hirsch, Robert O., 85
Holler, Frederick L., 98

ICPSR (Inter-University Consortium for Political and Social Research), 72, 74, 92
Irish, Marian D., 6

Jackson, Dorothy Lee, 67
Jennings, W. Pat, 82
Joint Center for Political Studies, 64, 92
Jones, Caroline D., 81
Jones, Charles O., 28

KTO Press, 36
Kaid, Lynda Lee, 85
Kaminsky, Laura J., 41
Kerwood, John R., 29
Kovenock, David, 73

Laboratory for Political Research, University of Iowa, 74, 92
Lazarsfeld, Paul F., 73
Library of Congress, 40
Lockheed Missiles and Space Company, 28
Long, Mary Jo, 82
Louis Harris and Associates, 87, 92
Lu, Joseph K., 99

McKibben, Carroll L., 73
McPhee, William N., 73
Marquis Academic Media, 65
Marquis Who's Who, 64
Mason, John Brown, 98
Matthews, Douglas, 63
Maxson, Wayne C., 103
Meyer, Evelyn S., 97
Michigan Senate Fellows, 29
Miller, Warren E., 73
Minnesota Historical Society, 71
Morehead, Joe, 97
Morris, Dan, 66
Morris, Inez, 66

Nabors, Eugene, 98
National Archives and Records Administration, 36, 102
National Observer, 30
National Opinion Research Center, 73, 87, 92
National Women's Political Caucus, 65
New York Times, 29
Newspaper Enterprise Association, 30
Newspaper Indexing Center, 30

O'Leary, Michael, 73
Oleszek, Walter, 5
ORBIT, 39

Palic, Vladimir, 99
Paul, Barbara D., 82
Peltason, Jack W., 6
Predicasts, Inc., 28
President's Commission on Federal Statistics, 57
President's Domestic Council Committee on the Right of Privacy, 59
Press, Charles, 87
Price, Miles O., 96
Privacy Protection Study Commission, 59

Prothro, James W., 6
Public Affairs Information Service, 40

Ralph Nader Congress Project, 65
Research Libraries of the New York Public Libraries, 40
Richardson, Richard J., 6
Ripley, Randall B., 5, 28
Rips, Rae Elizabeth, 97
Rosembloom, David, 85

Sanders, Keith R., 85
Scammon, Richard M., 70
Schmeckebeir, Laurence F., 97
Secretary of the Senate, 40, 41, 81, 83, 93
Sessions, Vivian S., 74
Shannon, Michael Owen, 97
Smith, Dwight L., 72
Sobel, Robert, 62
Stokes, Donald E., 73
Survey Research Center, 73–74
System Development Corporation, 39

Terry, Paul, 86
Thomen, Harold O., 40
Tolchin, Susan, 65
Tompkins, Dorothy L. C., 29
Turabian, Kate L., 103

Ujifos, Grant, 63
United Nations Association of the United States of America, 73
U.S. Commission on the Operation of the Senate, 72
U.S. Congress, 61, 62
U.S. Congress. House, 5, 33, 34
U.S. Congress. House. Clerk of the House of Representatives, 41, 70, 82, 89
U.S. Congress. House. Commission on Information and Facilities, 94
U.S. Congress. House. Committee on

Government Operations, 13, 57, 102

U.S. Congress. Joint Committee on Printing, 66

U.S. Congress. Senate, 5, 33, 34

U.S. Congress. Senate. Committee on Government Operations, 5, 10, 14, 59, 102

U.S. Congress. Senate. Committee on Government Operations. Ad Hoc Subcommittee on Privacy and Information Systems, 10, 102

U.S. Congress. Senate. Committee on Rules and Administration, 5

U.S. Congress. Senate. Committee on Rules and Administration. Subcommittee on Privileges and Elections, 80

U.S. Congress. Senate. Historical Office, 28, 93

U.S. Congress. Senate. Secretary of the Senate, 40, 41, 81, 83, 93

U.S. Congress. Senate. Select Committee on Presidential Activities, 80

U.S. Congress. Senate. Subcommittee on Constitutional Rights, 57

U.S. Department of Commerce. Bureau of the Census, 70, 72, 76–79, 88, 90

U.S. Department of Health, Education and Welfare. Secretary's Advisory Committee on Automated Personal Data Systems, 57, 103

U.S. General Accounting Office, 57–58, 91

U.S. Library of Congress, 40

U.S. Library of Congress. Congressional Research Service, 33

U.S. President, 103

U.S. President's Commission on Federal Statistics, 57

U.S. President's Domestic Council. Committee on the Right of Privacy, 103

U.S. Privacy Protection Study Commission, 59

University of Chicago, 104

University of Iowa, Laboratory for Political Research, 74, 92

Vose, Clement E., 99

Wall Street Journal, 30

Washington Monitor, 34, 35

Weinhaus, Carol, 99

West Publishing, 35

Wilcox, Allen R., 29

Williams, Oliver, 87

Wise, David, 6

Woodbridge, Mark, 41

Wynar, Lubomyr R., 71

Young, James S., 66

Zinn, Charles, 5

Zuckerman, Amelia, 66

Zuckerman, Ed, 66

Title Index

ABC POL SCI, 27

ABS Guide to Recent Literature in the Social and Behavioral Sci- ences, 27

The Almanac of American Politics: The Senators, the Representatives—Their Records, States and Districts, 62

America: History and Life, 27–28, 71

American Academy of Political and Social Science, the Annals, 27, 70

American Election Panel Study: 1956, 1958, 1960, 73

American Journal of Political Science, 27

American Political Parties: A Selective Guide to Parties and Movements of the 20th Century, 70

The American Political Process: Selected Abstracts of Periodical Literature (1954–1971), 71

American Political Science Research Guide, 27

American Political Science Review, 27

American Politics Quarterly, 27

American Statistics Index: A Comprehensive Guide and Index to the Statistical Publications of the U.S. Government, 77

America Votes: A Handbook of Con- temporary American Election Statistics, 69

Annals of the American Academy of Political and Social Science, 27, 70

Annals of the Congress of the United States, 34

The Annual Statistical Report of Contributions and Expenditures Made during the 1972 Election Campaigns for the U.S. House of Representatives, 81

The Annual Statistical Report of Receipts and Expenditures Made in Connection with Elections for the U.S. Senate in 1972, 82

Bibliographic Guide to Government Publications: U.S., 39

Bibliographic Tools: Volume II, Legislative Guide, 99

A Bibliography and Indexes of United States Congressional Committee Prints: From the Sixty-Fifth Congress, 1917, through the Ninety-First Congress, First Session, 1969, Not in the United States Senate Library, 41

A Bibliography and Indexes of United States Congressional Committee Prints: From the

Sixty-First Congress, 1911, through the Ninety-First Congress, First Session, 1969, in the United States Senate Library, 41

Bibliography of Publications, 1941–1960: Supplement, 1961-December 1971 (National Opinion Research Center), 87

A Bill to Establish a Federal Privacy Board, 8, 102

A Bill to Safeguard Individual Privacy from the Misuse of Federal Records and. . ., 7, 101

Biographical Characteristics of the United States Congress 1789–1977, 73

Biographical Directory of the American Congress, 1774–1971, 62

Biographical Directory of the United States Executive Branch, 1774–1977, 62

Black Americans in Congress, 64

Bureau of the Census Catalog, 78

CIS/ANNUAL, 39, 42–44, 48–49, 56, 94

CIS Five-Year Cumulative Index, 1970–1974, 39

CIS/INDEX: Congressional Information Service/Index to Publications of the United States Congress, 37–39, 45–47, 59, 94, 99

CIS/INDEX User Handbook, 39

CIS U.S. Serial Set Index, 20

CPS (Center for Political Studies)(1970–1976) American National Election Studies, 73–74

CQ Almanac, 21, 24–25, 37–38, 42–45, 56

CQ Weekly Report, 21, 23–26, 37–38, 40, 42–47, 56, 59, 68–69

CRF Listing of Contributors and Lenders of $10,000 or More in 1972, 82

CRF Listing of Contributors of National Level Political Committees to Incumbents and Candidates for Public Office, 81

CRF Listing of Political Contributors of $500 or More, 81

C.S.D. Advance Locator, 62

C.S.D. Election Index, 62

Calendars of the United States House of Representatives and History of Legislation, 34, 37–38, 43–47, 59

California News Index, 30

Candidate Name and Constituency Totals, 1824–1972, 74

Cannon's Precedents of the House of Representatives of the United States, including Reference to Provisions of the Constitution, the Laws, and Decisions of the United States Senate, 6

Capitol Hill Manual, 5

Catalog of Government Publications of the Research Libraries of the New York Public Libraries, 40

Changes in Congress, 29

Chicago Tribune, 30

Citation Manual for United States Publications, 104

Citizens Look at Congress, 65

Commerce Business Daily, 28

Congress: Process and Policy, 5

Congress and the Nation, 1945–1976, 24–25

Congress in Print: A Weekly Alert to Just-Released Committee Hearings, Prints and Staff Studies, 35

Congressional Attitudes toward Congressional Organization, 73

Congressional Digest, 27, 40, 46

Congressional Directory, 20, 62

Congressional District Data Book, 72, 77

Congressional Districts in the 1970's, 23, 77

Congressional Globe, 34

Congressional Index, 32–33, 37–38, 43–47, 59, 94

Congressional Insight, 24

Congressional Investigation of Lobbying: A Selected Bibliography, 29

Congressional Monitor, 34, 38, 46–47, 59, 94

Title Index

Congressional Pictorial Directory, 66

Congressional Procedures and the Policy Process, 5

Congressional Record, 4, 12, 15, 21, 28, 32–38, 43–47, 49–51, 53, 55, 59, 100

Congressional Record, Daily Digest, 43, 48, 50

Congressional Roll Call, 25, 37–38, 44–45

Congressional Rosters, 74

Congressional Sourcebook Series, 58

Congressional Staff Directory, 63

Congressional Studies, 27

Congressional Yellow Book: A Loose-Leaf Directory of Members of Congress, Their Committees, and Key Aides, 67

Congressmen and the Electorate: Elections for the U.S. House and President, 1920–1964, 75

Constitution, Jefferson's Manual and the Rules of the House of Representatives, 5, 20

County and City Data Books, 72, 77

The Cumulated Indexes to the Public Papers of the Presidents, 36, 44

Cumulative Index of Congressional Committee Hearings, 40, 43

Cumulative Index of Congressional Committee Hearings (Not Confidential in Character) from Seventy-Fourth Congress (January 3, 1935) through Eighty-Fifth Congress (January 3, 1959) in the United States Senate Library, 41

Cumulative Subject Index to the Monthly Catalog of United States Government Publications, 1900–1971, 39, 44, 56, 99

Cumulative Subject Index to the P.A.I.S. Annual Bulletins, 1915–1974, 40

Daily Operations of the United States Senate, 1975, 72

Database Catalog (Lockheed DIALOG Service), 28

Democracy under Pressure, 6

Democratic Review, 27

Deschler's Precedents of the United States House of Representatives, 5

Digest of Public General Bills and Resolutions, 33, 37–38, 43, 45–48, 54

Directory of Data Bases in the Social and Behavioral Sciences, 74

Directory of Federal Statistics for Local Areas: A Guide to Resources, 1976, 88

Directory of Government Documents Collections and Librarians, 95

Directory of Non-Federal Statistics for State and Local Areas: A Guide of Sources, 1969, 88

Directory of Registered Lobbyists and Lobbyist Legislation, 64

Draft Syllabus of Resources for Teaching Government Publications, 98

Editorial and Research Service, 25

Effective Legal Research, 96, 103

Elections and Electoral Behavior: A Bibliography, 71

Electoral Reform: Basic References, 80

FEC Disclosure Series, 84

Factual Campaign Information, 81

Federal Data Banks and Constitutional Rights: A Study of Data Systems on Individuals Maintained by Agencies of the United States Government, 57

Federal Election Campaign Act of 1971, 85

Federal Election Campaign Laws, 80

The Federal Index, 27–28

Federal Information Sources and Systems, 58

Federal Library Resources: A User's Guide to Research Collections, 95

Federal Program Evaluations, 58

Federal Register, 28

The Federal Register: What It Is and How to Use It; A Guide for the User of the Federal Register-Code of Federal Regulations System, 35
Federal Statistics, 57
The Federal Telephone Directory, 67
Financing the . . . Election, 82
Focus, 27, 63

GAO Review, 58
GPO Sales Publication Reference File, 39
Gallup Opinion Index Report: Political, Social and Economic Trends, 86
The Gallup Poll: Public Opinion, 1935–1971, 86
The Gallup Poll: Public Opinion, 1972–1977, 86
Government by the People, 6
Government Publications: A Guide to Bibliographic Tools, 99
Government Publications and Their Use, 97
Government Publications Review, 98
Guide to Congress, 5, 24
Guide to Current American Government, 25
A Guide to Library Resources in Political Science: American Government, 99
Guide to 1976 Elections, 68
Guide to Resources and Services, 1977–1978 (ICPSR), 72
Guide to U.S. Elections, 68

The Harris Survey Yearbook of Public Opinion, 87
Harvard Journal on Legislation, 27
Hind's Precedents of the House of Representatives of the United States, including Reference to Provisions of the Constitution, the Laws, and Decisions to the United States Senate, 6
Historical Abstracts, 72
Historical Election Returns, 1788–1976, 72, 74

Historical Statistics of the United States, Colonial Times to 1970, 71
House Journal, 4, 12, 33–34, 37–38, 43–45
House Manual, 5, 20
How Our Laws Are Made, 5

Impeachment and the United States Congress, 23
Implementation of the Privacy Act of 1974: Data Banks, 57
Index (National Observer), 30
Index of Congressional Committee Hearings (Not Confidential in Character) prior to January 3, 1935, in the United States Senate Library, 40
Index to the Christian Science Monitor, 29
Index to Congressional Committee Hearings in the Library of the United States House of Representatives prior to January 1, 1951, 41
Index to Legal Periodicals, 27
Index to Periodical Articles Related to Law, 27
Index to U.S. Government Periodicals, 27
Information Please Almanac, 30
The Information Sources of Political Science, 98
Inside Congress, 23
International Bibliography of Political Science, 28
International Political Science Abstracts, 28
Introduction to United States Public Documents, 97
Inventory of Information Resources and Services Available to the U.S. House of Representatives, Parts I-IV, 94

Journal of the Executive Proceedings of the Senate of the United States of America, 34
Journal of the House of Representatives of the United States of

America, 4, 12, 33–34, 37–38, 43–45

Journal of Politics, 27, 76

Journal of the Senate of the United States of America, 4, 12, 33–34, 37–38, 43–45, 102

Law and Contemporary Politics, 27

Leaders in Profile: The United States Senate, 66

Legislative History: Research for the Interpretation of Laws, 96

Legislative History of the Privacy Act of 1974, S. 3418, 59

The Legislative Process: A Bibliography in Legislative Behavior, 29

Legislative Studies Quarterly, 27

The Literature of Political Science: A Guide for Students, Librarians, and Teachers, 98

Los Angeles Times, 30

A Manual for Writers of Term Papers, Theses, and Dissertations, 104

A Manual of Style, 104

Materials Pertaining to S. 3418 and Protecting Individual Privacy in Federal Gathering, Use, and Disclosure of Information, 11, 102

Members of Congress since 1789, 23

Minnesota Votes: Election Returns by County for Presidents, Senators, Congressmen, and Governors, 1857–1977, 71

A Minority of Members: Women in the U.S. Congress, 64

Monthly Catalog of United States Government Publications, 35, 38–39, 43–44, 46–47, 56, 95

National Journal, 21, 26, 27, 37–38, 40, 44–47, 56, 59

National Roster of Black Elected Officials, 64

New Orleans Times-Picayune, 30

New York Times, 29, 47

New York Times Index, 29

News for Teachers of Political Science, 98

The Newsbank Urban Affairs Library, 30

The Newspaper Index, 29–30, 87

Newsweek, 87

1958 American Representation Study, 73

1940 Erie County Study, 73

1948 Elmira Study, 73

1948 National Election Study, 73

1944 National Election Study, 73

1975 Congressional Survey, 73

1974 Congressional Campaign Finances, 84

1972 Federal Campaign Finances, 83–84

1972 Federal Campaign Finances: Interest Groups and Political Parties, 84

The Official Associated Press Almanac, 30

Origins and Development of Congress, 23

Party Strength in the United States, 1872–1970, 77

Personal Privacy in an Information Society, 59

Political Campaign Communication: A Bibliography and Guide to the Literature, 85–86

Political Campaigns: A Bibliography, 81

The Political Marketplace, 85

Political Science Quarterly, 27

The Politics of American Democracy, 6

Polity, 27

Population Characteristics, P-20 Series, 78–79

Population Estimates, P-25 Series, 77–79

Powers of Congress, 23

Preservation, Protection, and Public Access with Respect to Certain Tape Recordings and Other Materials, 14, 102

Presidential Vetos, 1789–1976, 36, 38

Privacy: The Collection, Use and Computerization of Personal Data, 10, 102

Privacy, A Public Concern: A Resource Document, 58, 102

Privacy Act of 1974 (H. Rept. 93–1416), 13, 102

Privacy Act of 1974 (P.L. 93-579), 16, 55, 103

Public Affairs Information Service Bulletin, 24–25, 28, 40, 43, 45–47, 56

Public Interest, 27

Public Opinion, 86

Public Papers of the President of the United States, 36, 38, 44, 53, 103

Quadrennial Supplements to Cumulative Index of Congressional Committee Hearings (Not Confidential in Character): Quadrennial Supplement, together with Selected Committee Prints in the United States Senate Library, 41

RQ, 97

Reader's Guide, 87

Records, Computers and the Rights of Citizens, 57, 102

Referenda and Primary Election Materials, 74

Register of Debates in Congress, 34

Requirements for Recurring Reports to the Congress, 58

Research Resources: Annotated Guide to the Social Sciences, 98–99

Review: (year) Session of Congress and Index of AEI Publications, 26

Review of Politics, 27

The Role of Political Parties in Congress: A Bibliography and Research Guide, 28–29

Roster of Congressional Officeholders, 1789–1977, 74

Ruling Congress: A Study of How the House and Senate Rules Govern the Legislative Process, 65

SRC (Survey Research Center) American National Election Studies, 73

SRC Domestic Affairs Study, October, 1954, 74

SS Data: Newsletter of Social Science Archival Acquisitions, 74

Sacramento Bee, 30

San Diego Union, 30

San Francisco Chronicle, 30

Senate Journal, 4, 12, 33–34, 37–38, 43–45, 102

Senate Manual Containing the Standing Rules, Orders, Laws and Resolutions Affecting the Business of the United States Senate, 5, 20

Senate Procedure: Precedents and Practices, 5

The Serial Set, 19–20

Social Science Quarterly, 27

Social Sciences Citation Index, 28

Social Sciences Index, 28

Sources of Historical Election Data: A Preliminary Bibliography, 88

Staff Working Papers for Congressional Budget Scorekeeping, 58

State and National Voting in Federal Elections, 1910–1970, 68

State Blue Books and Reference Publications: A Selected Bibliography, 88

State Manuals, Blue Books and Election Results, 87

Statistical Abstract of the United States, 70

Statistics of the Presidential and Congressional Elections, 70

Statutes and Code: How to Find U.S. Statutes and U.S. Code Citations, 35

Studies in Money in Politics, 82

Studies in Political Finance, 82

Suggested List of Periodicals Useful for Legislative Reference Research, 28

Supplement to the Index of Congressional Hearings Prior to January 3, 1935, Consisting of Hearings Not Catalogued by the U.S. Senate Library, from the Twenty-Fifth Congress, 1839, through the Seventy-Third Congress, 1934, 40

Survey of Political Broadcasting, 84

Taylor's Encyclopedia of Government Officials: Federal and State, 66

Telephone Directory: United States House of Representatives, 66

Telephone Directory: United States Senate, 66

To Trace a Law: Use of Library Materials in a Classroom Exercise, 97

U.S. Census Data for Political and Social Research: A Manual for Students; A Resource Guide, 78

U.S. Code, 4, 12, 21, 35, 38

U.S. Code Congressional and Administrative News, 35–36, 37, 42–48, 51

U.S. Government Publications Relating to the Social Sciences: A Selected Annotated Guide, 99

U.S. Statutes at Large, 4, 12, 17, 21, 35–36, 38, 43–44, 48, 52–53

A Uniform System of Citation, 103

The United States Capitol: An Annotated Bibliography, 29

The United States Congressional Directories, 1789-1840, 66

United States Congressional Roll Call Voting Records, 1789-1976, 72, 74

United States Government Publications, 97

United States Law Week, 27

United States Political Science Documents, 28

The United States Senate: A Historical Bibliography, 28

Voting in Collegial Bodies: A Selected Bibliography, 29

Voting in Postwar Federal Elections: A Statistical Analysis of Party Strengths since 1945, 75

The Wall Street Journal Index, 30

The Washington Influence Directory, 66

Washington Information Directory, 93–94

Washington Monthly, 27

Washington Post, 28–30, 47, 87

Weekly Compilation of Presidential Documents, 4, 18, 21, 36, 38, 40, 44, 46–47, 49, 55, 103

Western Political Quarterly, 27

Who Was Who in American Politics: A Biographical Dictionary of Over 4,000 Men and Women Who Contributed to the United States Political Scene from the Colonial Days Up to and including the Immediate Past, 66–67

Who's Who in American Politics: A Biographical Directory of United States Political Leaders, 63

Who's Who in Government, 64

Witness Index to the United States Congressional Hearings 25th-89th Congress (1839-1966), 40

Women in Congress: 1917–1976, 64

Women in Public Office: A Biographical Directory and Statistical Analysis, 65

Women in the United States Congress, 1917–1972: Their Accomplishments; with Bibliographies, 64

Women's Political Times, 27, 65

World Almanac and Book of Facts, 30

Writing on American History, 28